W9-CSA-345

The Singer and His Art

The Singer and His Art

AKSEL SCHIØTZ

HARPER & ROW, PUBLISHERS • NEW YORK, EVANSTON, and LONDON

The music appearing on page 14 is taken from Benjamin Britten's *Canticle II, Abraham and Isaac,* Opus 51. Copyright 1953 by Boosey & Company Limited. Reprinted by permission of Boosey & Hawkes, Inc.

 For information address Harper & Row, Publishers, Inc., 49 East 33rd Street, New York, N.Y. 10016. Published simultaneously in Canada by Fitzhenry & Whiteside Limited, Toronto.

FIRST EDITION

LIBRARY OF CONGRESS CATALOG CARD NUMBER: 69-15259

To Gerd

Insist on yourself; never imitate. Your own gift you can present every moment with the cumulative force of a whole life's cultivation; but of the adopted talent of another you have only an extemporaneous half possession.

Ralph Waldo Emerson
Self-Reliance, 1841

Contents

Preface

Of all the arts, music is the most elusive and of all musical instruments the voice remains the most mysterious, even though it is part and parcel of our very selves. It is made of air. Although voices in some fashion were raised in song or psalm long before the harp or the drum was invented, the secret of their culture and production is still an enigma to all but a select few; for it must be said, if the truth be told, that there are more charlatans claiming qualification to teach voice culture than there are quacks in the medical profession. I am sure every singing teacher in the world will agree with me. The reason for this state of affairs is not hard to find: the student of an instrument can *hear* himself because the sounds he is making come from without; he can almost see—if he is a pianist or string player—whether or not he is making progress. For a singer to hear himself as others hear him is an impossibility. It is difficult for even the most experienced of artists to trust his own ears with certainty. He knows more by physical sensation whether he is placing his voice correctly or not.

It is small wonder that a young woman whose voice had been gradually deteriorating over the years replied, in answer to my enquiry as to her progress, "Madame is delighted with me. She tells me that I have great potentiality, that my voice is like a large mansion with many gorgeous salons and chambers, but at present these rooms are closed and shuttered. At the moment, Madame says, I am merely in the entresol of this mansion, and in two or three years all these wonderful rooms will be opened if I continue to take my lessons with her regularly."

I concede that Madame was a superb saleswoman, but I am afraid her misguided pupil has long since been disillusioned.

A bad teacher can ruin a voice. Is this young person forcing in the upper register, trying to turn herself into a lyric soprano when in reality she is a mezzo? This young fellow who is digging down to the bottom of the bass clef, is he not after all a light baritone? To give an authoritative answer to these questions is a very great responsibility, and only a pedagogue with knowledge and experience can supply it. He must assess the possibilities of the pupil's voice, tend it, place it, guard it from injurious habits.

Strangely enough there is no guarantee whatsoever that the artist who is or was a star of the operatic or concert platform, whose voice is beautifully produced, for whom technical difficulties do not exist, is able to teach or pass on his secrets to another. The fabulous Enrico Caruso, with his golden voice, and John McCormack, with his immaculate technique and breath control, were instinctive singers, destined to become great under any circumstances. I cannot imagine them giving lessons. Nor, I feel, would Melba or Tetrazzini or Chaliapin have had the long-suffering patience to iron out the troubles of a problem pupil. With all respect to these renowned singers and artists I cannot picture them as good teachers, for I do not believe they knew "the reason why." It is enough that they enriched the world, and we who heard them are thankful. I believe they would have passed on their secrets had they been able to do so.

It is my belief that most (but not all) of the best teachers of voice production were not notable performers. Pursuing this seeming anomaly into fields other than singing, one thinks at once of Leopold Auer and Theodore Leschetizky, famous to this day as pedagogues rather than as performers of their respective instruments—violin and pianoforte. Ernest Hutcheson, in New York, and Tobias Matthay, in London—to carry the argument further—are remembered today as teachers, not as executants.

Why then does Aksel Schiøtz, a great performer with an international reputation in opera and concert, with Lieder recordings which are a model for all singers (his *Die schöne Müllerin* is considered by many to be the finest record yet issued of this Schubert song cycle), differ from the other superb artists to whom I referred as instinctive singers?

In my opinion, Aksel Schiøtz owes his profound knowledge of the voice and the mysterious components that contribute to its production to a breakdown in health that quite suddenly struck him down. (This disaster overtook him on the very eve of a comprehensive tour of the United States. The impresario wrote me from New York, "I regard the advent here of Schiøtz as the most exciting artistic event I have ever handled in my life.") To put it brutally, this illness deprived Schiøtz of the power to walk or talk. The young singer, musically and vocally mature, with the world at his feet, found himself in the twinkling of an eye without a voice. After a long interval of convalescence, his health was restored. The problem now was to rediscover the singing voice. It is not for us to speak here of the courage this involved. It is enough that the problem was solved only after long and trying application. From a precious jewel, the voice had become a rough and uncut stone. It had to be dug out and polished. Schiøtz had to start again from the beginning. In testing this method and that method to coax his voice back to its natural beauty of tone and freshness, in working to regain muscular control of his breathing apparatus for steady emission of sound, in persuading the vocal stream into its right and proper channel, Schiøtz must have learned more than he ever knew before his illness about the workings of the voice.

Schiøtz is in an unequaled position to give factual evidence of vocal production. This book, written with the clarity, simplicity, and honesty that are characteristic of the man, will be of the utmost benefit to all singers and all lovers of beautiful singing. It is not, as the author emphasizes, a substitute for the student's singing lessons, but it should be on his bookshelf for constant reference as a supplementary aid to those lessons.

Many books have been written on this highly formidable and

controversial subject, but I know of none that carry the authority and intimate knowledge of this one. It will be regarded for years to come as a standard work.

Gerald Moore

Acknowledgments

Many people have helped to bring this book into being, and it is impossible to thank them all individually. However, special thanks should go to the University of Colorado, which supported my researches at the Music Library of the University of Oslo, Norway, with its famous Odd Udbye Collection of Schubert's songs.

Mr. Gerald Moore has done me the invaluable favor of writing the Preface and shows a true understanding of my own case as well as an uncompromising attitude toward the singer's art.

The master classes I gave at the Mannes College of Music, at the Aspen Music Festival in Colorado, at Miss Lola Hayes's studio in New York, and at colleges all over the United States furnished me with the experiences that I tried to put down in this book.

Mr. Earl Price gave me the benefit of his comprehensive knowledge of recorded music and helped me put together the list of recommended listening.

By her invitation to me to write about the interpretation of song, Miss Virginia Hilu, my editor, has shown great enthusiasm and an unfaltering wish to help me arrange my thoughts in a language that is not my mother tongue.

AKSEL SCHIØTZ

New York, September, 1969

Introduction

Music, vocal as well as instrumental, comes to life only when performed and interpreted. The great artistic value of the voice as a musical instrument and its ability to carry a message of beauty from heart to heart are the core of my exposition.

The "one and only method of singing" is a delusion and will not be given here. Breathing and producing sound are initially *unconscious* functions that have to be made *conscious* in the teacher's studio. *Singing as an art* can not be approached before the mastery of *singing as a skill.* My own "tools" for singing and teaching are described in the first chapters of the book.

I have made no attempt at historical completeness, but only weighed the possibilities in the vocal music of all periods *from the interpreter's point of view.* For most songs or arias, I have suggested available recordings by great artists, illustrative of my point, without any "music criticism" of composition or performer.

It is my hope that my own experiences as a performer may help the young singer who has the courage to enter this precarious profession.

The Singer and His Art

I

The Functioning of the Voice

The aim of this little volume is to give my ideas of the singer's art. You will not find in it a detailed exposition of singing methods and voice training, but I will try briefly to describe my own "credo," i.e., the way I myself use my voice and teach vocal technique. Ample information about voice physiology and technique can be found, for example, in William Vennard's book *Singing: The Mechanism and the Technic.**

The basic function of producing sound with the human vocal instrument is a simple one. In some wind instruments—the bassoon or the oboe, for example—an air current is pressed between two membranes, causing a vibration. The faint rattle or wheeze produced by the vibration is then amplified by the reverberations of the air in the various resonators. In the human body, air passes constantly through membranes—the vocal cords—when we breathe and renew the air in the lungs. When the air is exhaled between the membranes, and when the brain gives the signal to bring these together, the vibrating air enters the resonance rooms: the sound box or larynx, where the vocal cords are located, the pharynx, and the mouth cavity. A sound has been born! Compare the functioning of this mechanism to that of the antique automobile horn, which consisted of a rubber ball, a long, shiny brass tube, one or two membranes, and a winding trumpet. One produced a "honk" by pressing the rubber ball. The rubber ball corresponds to the lungs, which contain a certain quantity of air all the time; the brass tube corresponds to the windpipe (trachea); the membranes, to the vocal

* Los Angeles: University of Southern California Press, 1964.

cord; and the trumpet, to the mouth cavity and the other resonance rooms.

In the human vocal instrument, the squeezing or pressing is done by the diaphragm and the abdominal muscles. The diaphragm is the large, horizontal, lid-shaped muscle that separates the lungs from the abdomen. In the process of inhaling, it flattens and thereby allows the lungs to be filled with air. In exhaling, it curves upward and presses the air out of the lungs. Whether you speak, shout, or sing, the same process takes place. This process is unconscious and seems utterly simple, but when we try to find out *how* we do it, we realize that sound is produced by an extremely complicated mechanism. A singer must learn to breathe consciously and still remain natural and simple. If he does not, serious complications will inhibit a free and flowing tone. *Breath control,* both in exhalation and in inhalation, together with the proper use of the *resonance room* constitute the two most essential factors in producing a beautiful tone. The difference between speaking and singing lies in the use of pitch. In singing, the pitch is fixed.

THE TRAINING PROCESS

The manner in which the human vocal instrument is supposed to work has been a controversial point since voice training began, and the teacher must spare his student confusing conceptions when he teaches breath control and tone production.

The term *vocal method* has almost come to define the one and only right way to teach voice. The "one and only" way does not exist! Only certain elementary details of voice training are generally accepted by all teachers.

It is one of the most demanding duties of the teacher to be able to study each pupil individually and decide which "method" is the best in each case. The teacher should *teach individually*.

In order to develop the student's own personality so that he does not become just an assembly-line copy of his teacher, he must be taught to take a critical attitude toward everything he is told, while simultaneously developing confidence in his teacher. In no other way will his training produce positive and significant results.

If the young singer has been able to withstand the various bad vocal influences that he may have had forced upon him during his early years, the teacher will find the further training of his voice relatively easy. But if he has been forced to sing in choirs, if he has been encouraged to make his untrained "innocent" voice sing too loudly, or if, without any sensible instruction, he has imitated the unnatural crooning coming out of the television set, irreparable damage may already have been done.

In order to learn how to maintain natural and easy breathing in singing, the young person should observe the way a baby breathes when it yells its head off and watch how its little tummy and diaphragm are working. Or he should watch primitive people dancing and singing or shouting at the same time. The diaphragms of their well-trained bodies are very busy indeed. In order to experience this primitive way of breathing, you may hold a board or a big book over your head with both arms and breathe in and out, s-l-o-w-l-y, several times. By doing this, you will be prevented from what is popularly called "high breathing" (raising the shoulders and expanding the upper ribs of the chest cavity). Automatically, the abdominal muscles, the diaphragm, and the lower ribs are put to work. After a little while the board will seem as heavy as a slab of concrete or iron. Put it down, and the same breathing exercise will seem much easier.

Another exercise in which your diaphragm and abdominal muscles will be active consists of moving your stretched arms vertically from their hanging position along your sides out and up to their uppermost reach while inhaling; then down the same way while exhaling, both movements slowly. A good erect posture is absolutely necessary for low breathing.

One would think that relaxation would be a simple matter. But again and again beginners are stiff and tense in their efforts to do all the various things their teachers want them to do. The attentive teacher should instruct the student to let his shoulders sag, wag his head to and fro, and walk about the room in an almost "collapsed" manner. When the student realizes that tone production is becoming easier, relaxation will gradually become second nature to him. My swimming teacher told me again and again to be lazy, bodily lazy like the fish, in order to do the swimming movements in the most advantageous way. This advice applies to singing, too. Any tenseness anywhere will affect tone production and must be avoided wherever possible.

Try standing flat against a door or a wall. Make sure your heels, the small of your back, your shoulders, the back of your hands (thumbs away from you), and the back of your head are all touching the door. Then walk slowly forward trying to maintain this posture, without stiffening. Walking around the room, the whole body should automatically become relaxed.

Control of an even flow of the breath is best attained by practicing the so-called *messa di voce,* an Italian expression literally meaning the "sending out of the voice." It consists of producing a tone on a certain comfortable pitch with rising and falling dynamics: Make a long and even *crescendo* followed by a long and even *diminuendo.* This is much more difficult than you would think, especially the *diminuendo,* but it will help you attain a fine living tone.

The most challenging part of teaching tone production is teaching the student to use the resonance rooms to produce the most beautiful tone. There are many different conceptions of what a good and beautiful tone is. There is general agreement that it must contain certain aesthetic qualities besides the technical ones. A beautiful tone must flow freely and uninhibitedly on its way from the singer to the listener. It does not need the resonance rooms for amplification alone, but also for building a vault or dome over the tone to make it round and mellow.

Dynamically, a beautiful tone must be able to grow to a *fortissimo* without strain, and it must still be able to ring in a *pianissimo.* A beautiful tone must have some vibrato without allowing this vibrato to become a "wobble," i.e., spread over several notes, blurring the pitch. A beautiful tone must be able to adopt all kinds of shades and colors in order to be a ready tool for the singer to express every emotion or idea.

A more detailed look at the resonance room may be useful. Picture the mouth cavity, the main resonator, as a room with one big door and two smaller ones. The big door is the mouth opening, and it can be widened or narrowed by raising or lowering the jaw and shaping the lips for the various sounds of articulation. One small door leads "up" to the nasal cavity and the other "down" to the windpipe and the food pipe (esophagus). The jaw is the floor of the room, and on the floor there is a rug: the tongue. (Most of the time it should stay down where rugs belong.) The cheeks are the two side walls. The back part of the room is the pharynx, and the ceiling consists of the palate, hard in front and soft farther back (velum). When we sing, this room must be made as big as the various vowel sounds permit.

The jaw should be allowed to drop or sag. The tongue should lie flat and relaxed whenever possible. It should never be "swallowed" and allowed to fill up the throat. The tongue is a very agile muscle capable of assuming all kinds of shapes and positions; it is an aid in articulating the various consonants and vowels. When learning how to control your tongue, stand in front of a mirror and simply watch it while you speak.

When we yawn, the pharynx is expanded, and the singer experiences a slight "yawning sensation" when he sings.

The role of the palate, the ceiling of this flexible room, is a most important one. You cannot direct the air current to any particular point you want. "Placement of the tone" is an illusion. Sensations, however, play an important part in all tone production and formation, and the sensation of trying to make the breath hit the hard palate is helpful in making the tone intense, ringing, and well projected.

The main function of the soft part of the palate is to close off the mouth in its lowest position in order to let the air current pass to the nasal cavity. This is what happens when you want to pronounce the French nasal vowels. Together with the expanded pharynx, a slightly raised soft palate helps make the tone round and mellow. In a room with a flat ceiling, the tone will be shallow and lifeless.

Again, remember that you cannot learn to sing from a book. Only the teacher, the guide, can help you decide in which positions your various organs will produce the best tone. A recipe for success in singing does not exist, though some advertisers claim they have "The Only Way to the Bel Canto."

The student hears his own tone from "inside," and it is quite a different sound from what the "outside" listener hears. The tape recorder's playback often comes as a shock to the singer and can be very frustrating, but at the same time it can be most helpful. Scales, triads, and runs up and down the whole range of the voice are also helpful and necessary for "lubricating" and developing the voice. They should be done on all vowels in combination with various consonants under the teacher's guidance. Years and years of practicing scales and exercises exclusively, however, is detrimental and may kill the joy of making music, which is the final goal of singing.

Some of the seventeenth- and eighteenth-century Italian songs, particularly "Caro mio ben" (Giordani), "Amarilli mia bella" (Caccini), "Sebben crudele" and "Lasciatemi morire" (Monteverdi), "Verdi prati" and "Figlia mia, non pianger" (Handel), "Care e dolce" and "O, dolcissima speranza" (Scarlatti), make excellent "vocalises." Because they contain no complicated pronunciation problems, they serve the same purpose as exercises and scales. In addition, the English-speaking singer will profit from the pure and clear Italian vowels, which may have a most beneficial effect on his diction.

The teacher should concentrate his efforts on developing the musical personality of his student from the very beginning of his technical work with the voice. He should persist in trying to make the student project his own self in his singing. In forcing a certain "one and only vocal method," the teacher will appear autocratic and despotic and thus kill any sprouting artistic initiative the student may have.

TALENT

What is talent? Talent cannot be defined in a satisfactory way, but it can be recognized immediately. Hearing a talented singer is like being hit by an electric current. Talent colors the personal timbre of the voice and gives life to the expression of the song. Talent is something magic! In Greek mythology, the singer Orpheus, with his mysterious gift for moving stones, trees, and wild beasts with the sound of his voice, is the symbol of talent. Even the infernal deities were so moved by his singing that they allowed him to take his beloved Eurydice back to Earth from Hades.

Can talent be taught? It is not possible to teach an untalented person how to sing, but it is possible to bring out and develop a hidden talent. A happy combination of vocal and musical gifts and an inner sensitivity to music and poetry are the basic requirements for the student who wants to become a singer, but these qualities must be combined with a blend of humility and self-confidence, as the following examples will illustrate.

A young man wanted to sing for me, and his mother called and arranged for an audition. He was tall and handsome. His facial expression was of great confidence. His attitude toward the audition seemed to be, "Aren't you lucky to get to hear my beautiful voice? But, please, don't try to tell me anything, because I know I'm good!" It was obvious that his mother, who was going to accompany him on the piano, had been telling him since his earliest years that a second Caruso or Battistini was in store for the world.

The young man announced that he was going to sing "I Love You." He indicated neither composer nor poet, but started on Grieg's and Hans Christian Andersen's intimate "Jeg elsker dig."

His mother hurried through the short introduction just to give her wonderchild enough time to clear his throat and arrange himself in a heroic attitude. After an enormous heaving of the chest and shoulders, he lowered his head and bellowed the first phrase (which is marked *piano*.)

His face turned crimson, and the veins of his neck stood out like thick cords. Paying petty attention to the rhythmical pattern of the song, he hung on to every high note, completely distorting the intentions of the composer. Between phrases he took big breaths, and after the last high note the final line ebbed out into nothing.

Mother and son turned to me, their expressions showing that they expected an outburst of enthusiasm. I had to think fast, for in this short song the singer had demonstrated all kinds of technical, musical, and artistic errors. I thanked them both for the performance and for soliciting my judgment and suggestions. As diplomatically as possible, I explained how I thought the song should be performed.

Basically the boy had excellent vocal potential, but he was lacking in almost everything that makes a singer an artist: musical taste, musicianship, respect for the composition, an understanding of the poem, a balance between vocal strength and interpretation, and the ability to listen to the accompaniment and cooperate with the accompanist. Most serious of all was his "know-better" attitude, an attitude that would have to be changed before he could develop into a serious student. Humility is essential.

But I have encountered the opposite case as well. A shy young girl with a barely audible speaking voice wanted an audition. She was frightened and lacked self-confidence. It took her a long time to concentrate on what she was singing, but her pure bell-like soprano and rare musicianship revealed exceptional talent. Her delicate sensitivity made every phrase live. In her case, humility and shyness might well ruin a promising career. A certain amount of self-confidence is essential, too.

Between these two extremes one finds all kinds of combinations in the attitudes of students. A healthy balance must be worked out, and a mutual understanding between student and teacher should develop as they work to discover how the singer should use his voice and develop his artistic possibilities, his talent.

MUSICIANSHIP

One more important prerequisite to mastering the huge body of vocal literature is *musicianship*.

What is meant by musicianship? I believe that it contains four basic elements: rhythm, pitch, tempo, and dynamics. Can musicianship be cultivated? If so, how? Isn't musicality, like talent, something inborn? Isn't it either there or not there? Yes, but it may be hidden or underdeveloped, and in such a case I believe that studying can bring it out.

Go and learn to play an instrument! Learn to play the piano, the violin, or the flute. This may seem an odd piece of advice to give a singer, but the singer will soon find that it is easier to learn a song or an aria if he acquires some musical training by learning to play an instrument. His own inbuilt instrument, the voice, will become more obedient to his musical intentions. He will learn how to make his voice loud and soft, fast and slow, staccato and legato; he will learn how to make an accelerando or ritardando. By learning to play a string instrument, he will train his ear to be acutely sensitive to pitch.

Rhythm is the backbone of music. With a slight alteration of the Bible's "In the beginning was the Word," we could say, "In the beginning was rhythm." Rhythm is the element that all music, from the most primitive tribal forms to the avant-garde music of today, has in common. If a piece of music has no rhythm, it is a body without its skeleton, amorphous jelly.

To get the true feeling of a pulsating beat, you must have a metronome *inside yourself*, not on top of your music cabinet. Don't beat time with your hands, toes, or head. If you play or sing simultaneously with a metronome, you will neither develop your own rhythmical sense nor learn to produce sounds with the slightest resemblance to art. The mechanical beat of the metronome will kill any kind of living phrasing.

The metronome is a useful indicator of the tempo at which the composer intended his work to be played, but stop the metronome before starting the music, please! Some music, Samuel Barber's "I Hear an Army" (metronome marking: ♩=116 and ♩=84) for example, is impossible to sing to a metronome's beat. Most composers during the last hundred years have given a metronome figure, but in music composed before about 1850, your sense of style and musicality will have to suggest the tempo.

The suggested metronome markings in this book are only approximate. Automatically you will sing anything at a slower tempo in a bigger hall or in a church. Even the temperature may affect your tempo.

Exact pitch, naturally, is the first commandment for a singer, yet blurred pitch is often condoned if the voice is beautiful and appealing. Singing even slightly off pitch should never be tolerated. Technical imperfections often cause faulty pitch. Insecure pitch may stem from a "wobble," which is a too-pronounced vibrato. Tension is often the explanation for sharpness in pitch.

It is vital to find the right tempo for a song. A song will change character completely if it is done too fast or too slowly. All life and structure will disappear if it is sung too slowly, and it may lose its finer points and miss its whole intention if it is rushed through at breakneck speed.

One of the true marks of a genuine musician is the ability to arrive at just the right tempo for a song. Still more essential is whether a song is felt in two beats to the measure or in four, in one or in three, in two or in six, etc.

It is often very tempting to do the wonderful long legato line of a Brahms song slowly. In a song like Brahms's "Wie Melodien zieht es mir" (As Melodies It Draws Me), try beating the measure first in four and then in two. It may seem too fast in the double tempo. If you can still retain the idea of its indication, *zart* (tenderly), you will suddenly realize that this was what Brahms had in mind when he wrote the signature *alla breve* (cut time).

The metronome gives us the exact time and beat, but what is more important for the artistic performance of a song is the living rhythm and pulse. Glenn Gould, one of the greatest piano artists of today, was once asked if a certain pianist did not show a most fantastically crisp and chiseled rhythm in his virtuosolike playing of a work by Prokofiev. "Let him play a very slow movement to prove for us his sense of rhythm" was the pianist's answer. If you listen to Glenn Gould's own rendering of some of the very slow "Goldberg" Variations by J. S. Bach, you will realize why this is so true. Take the introductory chords of Hugo Wolf's setting of Goethe's "Anakreons Grab" (Anacreon's Grave). The dotted quarter notes must very distinctly contain the pulse beats of the three eighths in order to establish the *sehr langsam und ruhig* (very slowly and calmly) tempo of the twelve eighths. Hugo Wolf wants these long phrases all through the song. That is why he didn't write 3/8 or 6/8, which might have given the melody a misleading and totally wrong "barcarole" character.

Every tempo has its own character. Instead of the usual Italian indication—allegro, moderato, lento, etc.—the composer sometimes designates mood (in any of several languages), e.g., "tenderly,"

"solemnly," "with ease," "jubilantly," "gaily," which helps the performer convey the character that the composer finds in the poem. It is up to the performer to decide what tempo will best express the characterization.

Most modern composers give very exact indications for both metronome speed and specific character, sometimes in elaborate words and often throughout the song, as illustrated in Alban Berg's "Im Zimmer" from *Seven Early Songs.* First he says *Leicht bewegt* (lightly moving) and later *Zeit lassen* (take it easy), and then still later *Zurück in Tempo* (back into the first tempo). In "Les Angelus," Debussy says *Modéré, avec un douceur triste* (moderately, with a sad mildness) and *Très doux* (very softly). In his "Cheveaux de Bois," he says *Allegro non tanto—joyeux et sonore* (not too fast —happily and sonorously), and *à tempo: le double plus lent* (in a double slow tempo). In "C'est l'Extase," he says *Lent et caressant —rêveusement murmuré* (slowly and caressing—dreamingly murmured).

The character of a song is also obtained by obeying the composer's indications of dynamics: *pianissimo, piano, mezzo piano, mezzo forte, forte, fortissimo.* Good musicianship depends to a large extent on observation of these indications. Too often a student ignores them because he "feels" that a *forte* here or a *piano* there is needed. What the musician "feels" is beside the point and reveals most frequently a lack of understanding. When you analyze a song, you will realize that the composer almost always had a reason for using these dynamic markings, and a certain mood in the text is created when they are followed. A good musician will learn that the composer is his friend and accomplice. If he follows exactly the composer's indications of speed, dynamics, and characterization, interpretation of the work will be facilitated.

Another way to develop musicianship—perhaps a more passive one—is to sing in ensembles. Choral singing forces you to listen to what is going on in other parts, for any choir director knows how important it is that each singer listen not only to the sound he himself is producing but also to the others, in order to achieve the perfect blend of sound. In addition, the discipline and responsibility of being one in a group is excellent training. There are hundreds of ensembles, but no matter which one you join, one of the most important conditions for success is your ability to listen to the other singers in the group.

The approach to singing in chorus is widely different from the approach to solo singing. As only one of many, you should try to sound like the others. The effect of all the sections of the choir singing together will always depend on the degree to which a perfect blend can be obtained. One of the aims of the choral conductor should be to make the individual members of his choir listen to each other and have them become as similar in sound and expression as possible.

The step from choir member to soloist is an enormous and hazardous one. The wise conductor gradually leads the talented choir member from smaller solo parts to larger ones. Only through graduated training will one win sufficient experience for the larger and more demanding solo parts. In the beginning it is a frightening experience for the young singer to stand alone outside the security of the choir and hear his own voice being carried above the orchestra. With experience, however, he will gain self-confidence, and he will develop the personal approach to his part that is the most essential element in an artistic performance.

The early vocal composers (Palestrina, Pergolesi, Monteverdi, Buxtehude, Bach, etc.) regarded the voice as an instrument, the most expressive instrument of all (listen to Palestrina's *Missa Papae Marcelli*).

The pianist, cellist, and clarinetist should, ideally, "sing" on their instruments. When you sing the duets, trios, and quartets of, say, Schubert, Mendelssohn, and Brahms, you are singing chamber music. A perfect example of this is Benjamin Britten's *Canticle II: Abraham and Isaac*. Not only do we hear the refined way in which

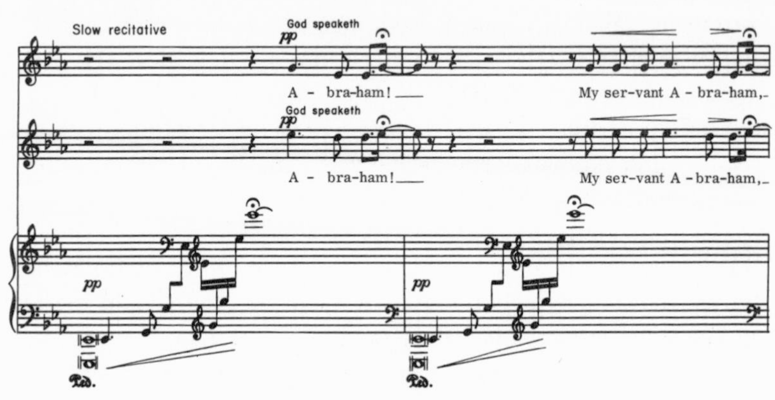

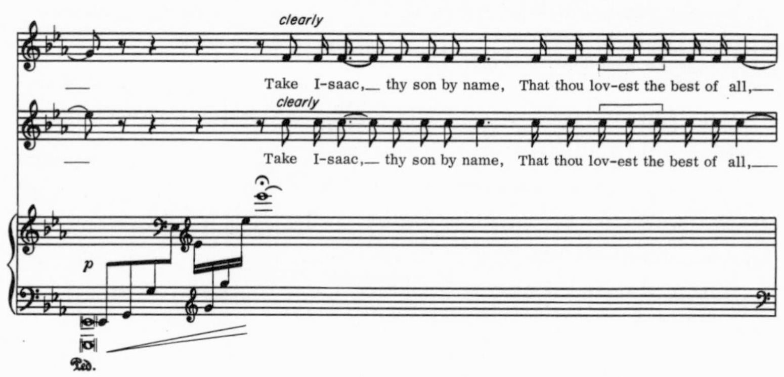

the contralto and tenor blend in duet, but at the beginning and end of the work the two voices, in the closest harmony, represent the voice of God, and the most ingenious sound effect is reached.

Musicianship also involves historical knowledge of the cultural and social structure of the world in which the composer lived and worked. This is a *sine qua non* for obtaining a sense of the style in the music of various periods.

Folk songs of all countries, from those of the dancing knights and noblewomen of medieval courts to the popular guitar-accompanied "folk singing" of today, should be sung in a seemingly nonprofessional manner, not sloppily, musically speaking, just freely and casually. You must try to give the impression of the layman singing for fun and love. Listen to Kathleen Ferrier, Richard Dyer-Bennet, Birgitte Grimstad, and Roland Hayes because their stylistic approach to the folk song is right.

The choralelike Bach songs from the *Schemelli Song Book* (1736) were sung with simplicity in the family circle of devoted pietists. They were never meant to be "performed" in front of an audience.

The *bergerettes* of eighteenth-century France must be done with an almost visual image of the prerevolutionary French aristocrats, artfully dressed as shepherds and shepherdesses. (Think of a painting by Fragonard.) You must understand their artificiality and stiltedness completely and still be able to evoke the freshness and charm of these rococo pastorales.

The so-called *Schubertiaden,* the regular gathering of Schubert's friends, was the true forum for his songs. They were not created with concert halls in mind. Johann Michael Vogl (outstanding and popular opera singer in Vienna, 1768–1840) and Schubert did the first performance of these songs with great taste and sensitivity.

All these different kinds of songs ask for as complete a knowledge as possible of their cultural background if the singer wants to avoid terrible stylistic misrepresentations.

II

The Art Song

INTERPRETATION, as it is defined in this book, stands for interpretation in solo singing and is the singer's personal approach to the vocal literature. "Interpretation" means to breathe life into the composer's work—nothing more. Solo singing occurs in three main categories: art song, oratorio, and opera. These categories are not always distinctly separated, and consequently the interpretative style can be difficult to discern.

Certain balladlike art songs have a "cast" that may seem to make them a sort of miniature opera without acting. Schubert's "Erlkönig" (Erl King) has four different characters, for example, Brahms's *Vier ernste Gesänge* (Four Serious Songs) is theoretically a Lieder cycle, but with its biblical texture it has some affinity to the oratorio category. By the same token some oratorios, Verdi's Requiem, for example, are operatic in their musical expression, and some operas lack stage action and are more like oratorios. Handel's *Giulio Cesare* is a good example of this.

The singer's interpretation in each of these categories should differ, as the descriptions of characteristic features of many art songs, oratorios, and operas, in this and the following two chapters, will illustrate.

The term "art song" is actually a misnomer because no justification at all could be given to any piece of music that is not art. But in America it is the traditional name for a poem set to music, a solo song accompanied by one or more instruments. The cheap and unoriginal "poetry" you often hear in popular songs can not pretend to belong to this category. The art song originated in the fifteenth and sixteenth centuries in Europe and was meant to be performed for the person who "paid the bill," the musician's patron. In the beginning, kings and princes sponsored this type of entertainment at their courts; later, the members of the audience themselves shared the expenses by paying admission. In our time the concert stage is the natural place for the art song.

The concert singer or recitalist who is asked to sing in an opera does not always know how to appreciate and take advantage of all the aids and facilities the theater offers him. And, vice versa, the opera singer often feels lost and almost naked when a concert grand is the only "property" on the stage, and then he must stand alone on the stage and in a very direct way "recite" the poems for his audience.

On the podium the singer has to do the whole "show," usually accompanied only by a pianist. Thus, the more rapport he can establish with his accompanist, the less lonely he will feel, and the better his chance will be of communicating with his audience.

Simple unaccompanied lays and songs of worship were man's first musical vocal utterances, and through romances or ballads of the medieval troubadours, minstrels, and storytellers, these developed into the art song as we know it today. The same personal feelings that were expressed in these early "la-la" scales and triads appear in the more complicated art song set to poetry.

Most likely the young singer will get in contact with this category when he first sings as a soloist.

Sometimes in my career as a concert singer I have succeeded in moving my audience with my interpretation of the poet's words and the composer's music. It was as if I were communicating their message, not to an audience of hundreds, but directly to a single person. This experience, when it occurs, which is not often, is the fulfillment of the concert singer's *raison d'être,* proof of his re-creative powers, proof, even, of his being a creative artist in his own right. Such a happy spiritual union between performer and audience is usually called a moment of inspiration. This word, however, does not quite explain what is actually taking place. The singer feels inspired by the words and the music; the audience is moved, uplifted, or carried away by his interpretation; and a rapport between singer and audience is established. The singer responds to the alertness of the audience, and their emotion has the effect on him of an electric current, driving him to give the utmost of his own vitality and personality.

The singer who fails to act as the humble servant of music and poetry and as the faithful messenger of composer and poet alike will never strike a spark with his audience. In bringing the songs he sings to life, the interpreter must feel his responsibility toward both composer and poet and their intentions as closely as possible. His artistic conscience should restrain him from augmenting or in any way distorting the composer's original intent about the way the poem should sound in his music.

A singer's personal style of interpretation involves many intangibles, but there are a few obvious characteristics that every singer must have. He must have a definite talent not only for singing but also for making the audience listen. It is not enough that his vocal cords should cause the sound to hit the listener's eardrums in a pleasant way; rather, he should arouse the listener's mental activity and emotions by the music that he tries to re-create. This talent can be supported and supplemented by those tricks of the trade or tactics that all singers have to learn.

He must have pleasant stage manners which always help put the audience in a responsive mood. Every performance is for the singer a battle to conquer his audience. This battle starts the minute he walks on stage. The crowd that meets him may be indifferent or passive, perhaps even a little negative. Or they may have come with such great expectations that they are disappointed in the first round, and the singer has to overcome this hurdle. If they find his stage manners bad to boot, he will have an even harder time winning them over.

Within less than two hours the singer has to convince his listeners of the importance of his message and then submit himself to the immediate impact of their judgment. In this very short time he must stir them to such an extent that they will forget such irrelevancies as his hairdo, dress, and gestures. All of these are, of course, part of the "game," but they must not distract attention from the singing.

The singer must be able to strike and maintain a balance between well-projected tone and well-articulated words. He will defeat his own aims if his text is indistinct. If he does not project the words, he will break the rapport, the power line, between himself and the audience. And yet he must take care not to chop the cantabile vocal line to pieces with the words. These should be clear and easy to understand, and convey the whole meaning of each phrase and each word.

"Warm love" and "beautiful girl" should not be sung in the same way as "cold hate" or "engine rattle." The singer must express the illusion that he feels warm love seeing the beautiful girl; otherwise he will not communicate the poet's feelings to the audience.

In the performance of art songs the singer must realize that the program, not he, is the focal point. He is nothing but the medium who brings the songs to the audience. He should always maintain this humble attitude. When he is before an audience, his principal goal should be to pass on to them a message of beauty in words and sound, not just to display his own vocal splendors. This attitude is fundamental to a conscientious interpreter and saves the singer from the dangers of superficiality, overinterpretation, and overdramatization. He will bore the audience if he understates the contents of the song and concentrates only on vocal facility. Again, he must strike a balance between dramatic expression and vocal performance.

To interpret actually means to explain. Thus, the singer should explain to his audience the contents of the poem by way of music. Singers are taught various means of presenting music to an audience. Facial expressions are essential; an immobile face will cancel out even the most beautiful voice. But only the singer's inner emotions should give rise to his facial expressions. Otherwise the audience will suspect that these expressions are not genuine, and the singer's chances of establishing a rapport with the audience will diminish. Gestures may be used, but they are dangerous; movements on the podium should be kept to a minimum and used only in very dramatic passages or when they spring spontaneously from the singer's emotions. More often than not they disturb and detract.

True interpretation comes from within. Only when the singer is fully aware of the contents of the poem is he able to tell the story in such a way that the audience is compelled to listen. Interpretation is, thus, a matter of a singer's own individuality and a result of his own personal experiences in life; through these he reflects the poet's words. His particular temperament and imaginative power furnish the essential coloring of the performance. If he has sufficient intelligence and sensitivity, he will understand the full meaning of the words and form his musical phrasing with these words as the inner core. He will never become stagnant in his work; rather, he will grow with repeated performances. He will discover new shadings, perhaps a whole new meaning in the words, or an entirely new phrasing of the music. Alfred Cortot, the great French pianist, declared that you don't know a composition until you have performed it a thousand times.

But there always remains the danger of overinterpretation. Any singer can become too subtle, too dramatic, too sentimental. A simple song must be performed with simplicity, yet it must never be boring. Actually, delivering a program of songs might be compared to walking a tightrope. The singer must continuously keep his balance by using the right proportions of expression, gestures, dynamics, vocal shadings, and so on. If he exaggerates, the rope will break; if he understates, the rope will slacken. In both cases he will fall. His musicianship and his artistic taste should constantly control his balance and yet give him sufficient freedom of movement to respond to the composer's indications.

In addition, he must always retain the freshness of his first reaction to a song. Even though he penetrates the poem and develops his own poetic ideas about it, that first bloom of innocence it had when he discovered it should never be allowed to fade. Retaining this freshness when one has had to repeat certain songs innumerable times is much more difficult than one might think.

The singer of today has an obligation to work hand in hand with contemporary song composers and try to interest the musical audience in new ideas and ways of expression. At the same time it is his privilege to tackle the great musical value of pieces from earlier periods. It takes both a sense of style and some courage to attempt to interpret music that was written several centuries ago.

There are fashions in music as in so many other-fields. Today a huge body of baroque music from the eighteenth century is being performed, recorded, and broadcast. The songs of Bach, Handel, Mozart, and Beethoven contain musical and aesthetic values that today's audiences understand and welcome.

The enormous treasures of "the song with piano" literature of the nineteenth century also speak to the hearts and minds of modern listeners. They are moved by the genuine emotions of the "arch-romantic" poetry in the songs of Schubert, Schumann, Brahms, Wolf, Mahler, Strauss, Berlioz, Duparc, Chausson, Debussy, Fauré, Ravel, Delius, Elgar, Vaughan Williams, Musorgski, Rachmaninoff, Rimski-Korsakov, Sibelius, and many others. The bubbling brook, the deep valley, the vast ocean, the dark forest, the bright sun, the blue flower, the green grass, warm love, cold hate, jealousy, despair, longing, sorrow, and joy are eternal phenomena and part of everyone's life. We still want to hear about them and to be moved deep in our hearts by them.

In the introduction to her book *More than Singing,** Lotte Lehmann says some wise things about interpretation. Interpretation is an expression of the individual personality, and cannot be taught or "put on you" by somebody else. "Imitation is the enemy of artistry," says this great interpreter. What can be taught or developed is the power of imagination. Lotte Lehmann recommends

* New York: Boosey & Hawkes, Inc., 1945.

simply that the singer register the reactions he has while reading the poem aloud and retain them when singing the song.

Her indications of interpretational behavior on the concert stage, however, contain a great danger for the inexperienced student. "Your eyes are half closed," "Your hands are folded," "Your head is thrown back," "Your body leans forward" may be excellent suggestions, but they should be only suggestions. Once I heard and saw one of Lotte Lehmann's students do all this exactly as her teacher had told her to do it, but she was completely awkward and artificial. Yet *More than Singing* remains one of my dearest treasures. To the experienced performer who has already experimented with his own ways of expression, the book is a marvelous inspiration.

In the studio the student, under his teacher's watchful eye, can experiment with expressing his feelings with his eyes, lips, hands, and body movements. He can try darker shades of voice for sorrow and lighter shades for joy, an almost breathy or veiled sound for longing, and a brassy and harsh sound for anger and fury. Again and again, though, remember that any suggestions made by the teacher are *only* suggestions. Interpretation must come genuinely from within the singer, or it will appear artificial.

A wonderful thing in Lotte Lehmann's book is the stress she puts on keeping the atmosphere the singer has tried so hard to create until the postlude of the song is finished. "Hold the tension all through the postlude," she says. Nothing wrecks the mood or is more disillusioning to the audience than the singer who shows too obviously his feeling of relief that his singing is ended and permits the pianist to play the postlude as fast as he can. "The song starts where the prelude starts and ends only when the postlude ends." This is a rule that every interpreter should keep in mind.

Whether you fold your hands, stand erect, turn your eyes down, or lean forward, you *must* hold the mood, into which you may have succeeded in taking your listener, to the very end of the song. If you have concentrated deeply on the contents of the song and have experienced the emotions it contains, no instructions in expression or gestures should be necessary. What is natural and true is easily perceived by the audience.

For this reason I believe fervently in master classes. In a master class the student has an audience of his fellow students who can always be depended upon to react spontaneously to any expressions or gestures that seem artificial. Because of their keen interest in and love for the art song, the critical and sometimes puzzling questions they ask may open a fruitful and essential discussion if it is well guided by the "master." It is important that not only active singing students participate in such a class, but also a number of auditors.

One question I have had to answer many times (and here I cannot agree with Lotte Lehmann) is, "Could this song, which was written for a woman, be sung by a man?" Or, in a sad tone from a female singer, "Is this a man's song?" already expecting me to answer in the affirmative.

Once, a fine, well-known soprano who is still with us gave a performance of Schumann's *Dichterliebe*. She produced wonderful sound and gave evidence of fine musicianship, but when she sang the lines "Wenn ich mich lehn' an deine Brust" (When I lean to your bosom) and "Wenn ich küsse deinen Mund" (When I kiss your [her] mouth), the discerning and understanding audience felt utterly revolted. I cringed, just as I would have if I had heard a man sing Schumann's *Frauenliebe und -leben*. The song's "Seit ich ihn gesehen, glaub' ich blind zu sein" (Since I saw him I seem to be blind), "Will in's Ohr dir flüstern alle meine Lust" (Will whisper into your ear all my joy), and "Weisst du nun die Tränen?" (Do you now realize why I cry?) were written to be sung by a woman about a man she loves and should never be sung by a man. There are certain hurdles the imagination just can't cross, and the Lieder singer should remember this when forming his repertoire. It is a poor excuse that the audience won't understand the words. A woman should definitely *not* attempt songs written for the male singer, and vice versa. I am positive that most poets would agree with me. It is the poet's work the composer and the performers are interpreting, and there are few poets who condone any change of sexes.

GERMAN LIEDER

WOLFGANG AMADEUS MOZART (1756–1791), FRANZ JOSEPH HAYDN (1732–1809), and LUDWIG VAN BEETHOVEN (1770–1827)

Without hesitation, I would call Mozart the greatest composer of all times. Palestrina, Bach, Handel, Wagner, and Verdi are sovereign in specific fields, but Mozart achieved all-around perfection in piano, violin, flute, string and woodwind quartets, symphonies, oratorios, operas, and songs.

Most of his songs are small dramatic scenes or arias like "Als Luise die Briefe ihres ungetreuen Liebhabers verbrannte" (When Louise Burnt the Letters from Her False Lover), but in his setting of Goethe's "Das Veilchen" (The Violet), written long before Schubert's time, all the elements of the Lied appear. This concise, crystal-clear miniature encompasses a whole world of love, longing, happiness, and tragedy with an accompaniment that ingeniously evokes the mood and atmosphere of Goethe's poem. In many respects it is a parallel to Schubert's "Heidenröslein" (Heath Rose), also a poem by Goethe.

The singer must describe in a concentrated form the modest, carefree, and self-sufficient little violet which suddenly becomes enamored of the beautiful, tripping shepherdess and her singing. The words "und sang" (and sang) could be slightly stressed and prolonged in order to introduce the melody of the accompaniment. The play on words between "Veilchen" (little violet) and "Weilchen" (little while) must be discreetly, but distinctly, brought

(Suggested MM: ♩=60)
Allegretto
Ein
Veil-chen auf der Wie-se stand, ge-bückt in sich und un - be -kannt: es war ein her-zigs Veilchen.
p
f
p
f
p

out. "Oh, I wish I were the most gorgeous flower so that she might notice me, if only for a *little while*." Try to avoid using Mahlerian or Straussian sentimentality in interpreting the tragic crushing of the lovely violet under the negligent foot of the shepherdess. Control your feeling of sorrow (for it *is* a tragedy) when you sing "es sank, und starb" (it fell and died). The thought that it is a joy to die at the hand (or under the foot) of your beloved is characteristic of the poetry of that period, but the singer should sing it with an "inner smile" in his voice (listen to Elisabeth Schwarzkopf).

The canzonettas and songs of Haydn also prepared the way for the more elaborate and significant accompaniment which is characteristic of the *Lied*.

During his visits to London in 1790 and 1794, he wrote songs with original English lyrics—among others, "She Never Told Her Love" (from Shakespeare's *Twelfth Night*). It is not a poem but some of the lines from the play, and it gives the singer an opportunity to sing free recitative—like phrasings inside the rhythmical pattern of Haydn's music. The accompaniment is very expressive, and it takes an excellent pianist to do full justice to the song.

"The Spirit's Song" (suggested MM: ♩=66) shows great imaginative power, and the performer must seek to express the warmth and love that lie in the phrases of the comforting deceased spirit. (Listen to Peter Pears with Benjamin Britten at the piano.)

For the English-speaking singer there is a rewarding field in these undeservedly neglected songs.

Beethoven's intense, introspective *Sechs Lieder* (Six Songs) by Christian F. Gellert provide a good preparation for singing in oratorio.

Beethoven did not have much compassion for the singer. He would not change one note (so the story goes) of the vocal quartet

(Suggested MM: ♩=66)
She sat, like Pa - tience on a mon - u-ment, smil - ing,
smil - ing at — grief, smil - ing,
smil - ing at grief.
f
mp
p
p
fp
fp

that ends his Ninth Symphony, even though the singers entreated him to do so because they found it unsingable. They were right. Unless you own a superhuman Wagnerian voice, you will be drowned out by the orchestra.

His cycle of six songs by Jeitteles, *An die ferne Geliebte* (To the Distant Beloved), is a real challenge for the performer. In all six songs, the poet longs for his beloved and wishes that his ardent love will be able to carry his songs to her. I find them very difficult to perform and not "vocal" at all. They could be done just as well by piano or violin solo.

The principal difficulty in performing *An die ferne Geliebte* is that the singer must be able to use several kinds of voice: a lyric cantabile for "Wo die Berge so blau"; an instrumental, quasi-pizzicato for "Leichte Segler in den Höhen"; and at the very end, a full, trumpet-like, dramatic voice for "was ein liebend Herz erreicht" (What a Loving Heart Can Reach). The *An die ferne Geliebte* cycle became the paragon of the song cycle so much in fashion at that time. With its various movements, it is as firmly constructed as a sonata or a symphony, and it is impossible and wrong to break the continuity (listen to Ernst Häfliger or Dietrich Fischer-Dieskau).

FRANZ SCHUBERT (1797–1828)

The songs of Schubert, in which the accompanist plays as great a role as the singer, have been the prototype of song writing ever since they were created. Schubert was deeply influenced by the Romantic movement in literature. The impact of nature upon human life and mood was one of the characteristics of the poetry of Romantic literature. The singer should be completely involved in the contents of the poem before he ventures to present it. The non-German singer should know not only the exact meaning of every word but also the connotation and the atmosphere of each word, each phrase, and finally of the whole poem.

Of the more than six hundred songs Schubert wrote, I will mention a few which are characteristic. Later in this chapter, the interpretational problems of his two cycles *Die schöne Müllerin* and *Winterreise* will be covered in more detail.

In "Schäfers Klagelied" (Shepherd's Lament), written in 1814, Goethe's shepherd wants to leave the hills because some inner longing draws him toward the valley; he does not quite know why, for *she* left that dear place long ago.

Though you may be tempted, you will find big rubati quite unnecessary, because Schubert has done it all for you in the accompaniment. The very calm 6/8 movement describes the grazing flock and the flowers of the meadows. The excitement of the rain,

wind, and storm is depicted by repeated nonlegato sixteenth-note chords. Sadness and hopelessness are the emotions that must be

expressed in this song, which is full of the characteristic freshness of Schubert's early work.

In "Frühlingsglaube" (Faith in Spring), written in 1820, we

picture Schubert reading about the mild spring breezes that work miracles in beautiful nature. His heart is caressed and comforted by the arrival of spring. He is overwhelmed by the poignancy of the line "Man weiss nicht was noch werden mag" (One does not know what is going to happen), and almost faster than he can write the notes, he hears the music in his mind. (He had no instrument of his own, and had to run to a friend to play and sing the final result.)

The performer must adhere to the strict form of the song. He must not become so overwhelmed by its beauty that it reflects his own feelings more than Schubert's. He must feel two beats to a measure and not four. Sing it *ziemlich langsam* (*somewhat* slowly), not *very* slowly. If you sing the dotted notes and appoggiaturas metronomically, you will impart a jerky, stilted character to the melody which is not in keeping with the idea of mild spring breezes. So you have to smooth the sharp corners without distorting the original rhythmical pattern. Few indications of dynamics are given, but the main indication (with Schubert, almost always in the accompaniment only) is *pianissimo* with a slight *crescendo* and *diminuendo* at the end of the first and second parts of the melody.

The worst thing that can happen to the pure and simple Schubertian song is to be performed as a "singer's number," i.e., in a theatrical manner. The operatic singer often thinks that he has to compensate for all the props of the operatic stage, which are lacking on the concert stage. He regards the piano introduction merely as a time for the audience to admire his formal attire and his appearance in general. He makes it quite clear that the introduction has nothing to do with the song. A long ritardando and fermata at the end of the introduction allow him time to pull himself together, fill his chest, take a step forward, and then. . . . He pays not the slightest attention to the "background music," which is all the piano part is to him. All that counts is how his own voice sounds and how he impresses the audience; the poor accompanist and poor Schubert suffer. On the other hand, marvelous musical

(Suggested MM: ♩=42)

taste is shown by Heinrich Schlusnus, Dietrich Fischer-Dieskau, and Fritz Wunderlich.

In "Wanderers Nachtlied" (Wanderer's Nightsong), written in 1823, "Über allen Gipfeln ist Ruh'" (suggested MM: ♩=42), Schubert's music matches the tranquil simplicity and beauty of the Goethe poem in the happy and genuine manner of the true genius. More than ever, the singer must be humble and try to present the creation of the two great men as honestly as possible (listen to Fischer-Dieskau).

In "Die Stadt" (1825), we have again a description of nature:

the fisherman in his small rowboat moving across the lake with the water dripping from the oars. Behind this idyllic picture lie the deep emotions Schubert experienced when he wrote the music. The confused and unhappy feelings of the jilted lover are the true contents of the song. Not water, but tears are dripping into the lake.

I suggest a dark, plaintive shade of voice when one sings about the town where *she* lives, all surrounded in mist and blurred, as by tears. The singer must express bitterness and despair (listen to Fischer-Dieskau).

In "Der Doppelgänger" (The Double), composed in 1828, the jilted lover is standing in the town where she lived in front of the house that used to be her home. He discovers a man standing there with his eyes fixed on her window. Suddenly he shudders; in the moonlight he sees the reflection of his own face. It must be either an apparition or his own double who is making all the gestures he used to make in the old days.

From the eerie stillness produced by the slow, somber chords of the introduction to the *fortissimo* shriek in measure 41, Schubert has written one long *crescendo* in which the listener can almost feel the heartbeat of the lover. Sorrow, horror, and despair should be expressed with a dark and sinister voice. Avoid false dramatizing. Even if you are tempted to let your own emotion add something by distorting the rhythmical pattern of the phrases, don't. Schubert's way was right!

In "Die Stadt" and "Der Doppelgänger," which are both poems of Heinrich Heine, Schubert was describing the same subject, loss of the beloved one, but what a variation of melodic themes and harmonies he has written! (Listen to Fischer-Dieskau).

Schubert wrote two cycles, *Die schöne Müllerin* (The Lovely Milleress, as Richard Dyer-Bennet charmingly translates it) and *Winterreise* (Winter's Journey). They consist of twenty and twenty-four songs respectively, with words by the composer's contemporary, Wilhelm Müller, whose lyrics do not match Heine's great poetry. In both cycles each song is a distinct entity, but Schubert in his instrumental accompaniment ingeniously creates a mood that suits the poetic feelings of the poems and builds a continuing atmosphere which makes song cycles of them. It is unfortunate to take a single song out of context, but this is often done. They are meant to be links of a chain, and it is a shame to break this chain. Paul Henry Lang says the following of the two cycles in *Music in Western Civilization*:*

> By consciously elevating such purely musical elements as harmony and instrumental accompaniment to equal importance with poem and melody, he brought to bear upon the atmosphere of the song the force of an overwhelming musical organism, a force sufficient to establish a balance between poetry and music.
>
> His instrumental accompaniment, especially in the songs of "Die schöne Müllerin" and "Winterreise," acts in a manner not unlike Mozart's opera orchestra, furnishing *the mood, the soil from which grows the vocal flower*. Hence, the uninterrupted enchantment of these song cycles; the accompaniment holds us permanently in the mood of the idea, while the voice, especially in the "Winterreise," gives us its various images.

Die schöne Müllerin was written in 1823 after Schubert had already created such miracles as "Gretchen am Spinnrade," "Erlkönig," "Heidenröslein," and about three hundred other songs. The tragic love story is universal and timeless with its half-classical, half-romantic musical pattern. The poems inspired Schubert to write immortal music, which expresses, better than the words alone, the emotions of the unhappy lover.

The young and inexperienced singer who wants to follow the directions given earlier in this book can learn a tremendous amount

* New York: W. W. Norton & Company, Inc., 1941, p. 780.

from thorough work with *Die schöne Müllerin.* He has a fair chance of doing justice to the songs about the naïve young miller, for it is a natural thing for a young man today to "be on the move," to get away from familiar surroundings, and to feel the wanderlust of the romantics.

Among the twenty songs, there are both simple and straightforward ones such as "Das Wandern," "Wohin?" "Danksagung an den Bach," "Morgengruss," "Des Müllers Blumen," and "Die liebe Farbe," and the more complicated ones such as "Am Feierabend," "Der Neugierige," "Pause," "Der Jäger," "Eifersucht und Stolz," and "Die böse Farbe." Simple songs are often the most difficult to perform because you get relatively little support from the composition itself, and the demands on the singer's interpretational and stylistic talent are rather great; whereas the violent emotions you have to express in the songs of a more intricate character lie, for the most part, in the accompaniment.

Briefly, here is the story of the cycle. The young miller follows his "friend" the brook, which leads him to the next watermill. He falls in love with the master miller's daughter and believes that she is in love with him, until he realizes that she loves the green huntsman and not the white miller. Sorrow and despair overwhelm him. He drowns himself. At the end the brook sings a lullaby over the dead miller.

The singer must express the excitement of the adventure that lies before the boy. The five stanzas of "Das Wandern" (Wandering) should be differentiated as much as possible. I suggest a fresh and gay *mezzo forte* for the first, a *piano* imitation of the murmuring of the running water in the second, for the third and fourth a heavy *forte* like that of the rumbling stones in the brook, and for the last a slight allargando, always paying due attention to the *pianissimo* echo effect at the end of each verse (suggested MM: ♩=80).

Since most of the songs of *Die schöne Müllerin* are strophical, you must pay attention to the contrast in your interpretation to avoid monotony in the constant repetitions.

The question in the title of the second song, "Wohin?" (Where to?), tells you that you have to express the boy's insecure state of mind. Two beats to the measure and a light use of the voice will give this charming trifle the right character (suggested MM: ♩=80).

The third song is titled "Halt" (Halt), and the accompaniment, with its opening *forte* phrase and the accented note in the second measure (as though to say "stop!"), illustrates this. The well-known

joy at the familiar should be clearly expressed in "und die Sonne wie helle vom Himmel sie scheint" (and how brightly the sun shines from the sky) in an almost caressing legato.

In "Danksagung an den Bach" (Thanksgiving to the Brook), the voice must be the sweetest possible in order to express the miller's overwhelming bliss and gratitude to the brook. Also, you will obtain the necessary lightness if you stress two beats to the measure in your phrasing (suggested MM: ♩=42).

In song number five, "Am Feierabend" (After the Day's Work), a boisterous and almost explosive singing (well within limits, of course) will express the boy's wish to show with what physical strength he loves the miller's daughter. "I wish I had a thousand arms and was as wild as the millstream in order to show her my ardent love." But, alas, she wishes a sweet goodnight to everyone, not to him alone. The master miller's phrases are low, and the girl's are high, so it would be wrong to try to imitate the bass and soprano voices. The very fact that Schubert indicates *etwas geschwinder* (somewhat faster) at the repeat justifies a slight ritard from "Und da sitz' ich in der grossen Runde" (and there I sit in the big circle), but this should be done in the interludes, so that the following vocal phrase becomes slower. Do not make any ritardando at the very end.

(Suggested MM: ♩. = 84)

Today's singer may find "Der Neugierige" (Curiosity), with its conversation between the young man and the flowers, the stars, and the brook, the most incompatible in the cycle. Still, of all Schubert's songs it is my favorite. The boy wants only one answer from the brook: Does she love me? Yes or no? His anxiety and curiosity are so marvelously expressed in the music that the best you can do is to follow Schubert's indications as closely as possible. In his time much phrasing was left to the musical taste of the performer, and I suggest a slight *crescendo* in the accompaniment leading to "Ja, heisst das eine Wörtchen" (Yes is the one little word), and then a *piano* chord before "Das andre heisset nein" (the other word is No).

If you keep strict time, both here and in the following two phrases, you will note that the weight is put at the end, "Die beiden Wörtchen schliessen die ganze Welt mir ein" (the two words encompass the whole world for me), which undoubtedly is where Schubert wanted it. I have never been able to understand the *piano* marking on the word "ganze." I suggest that it be moved to the following measure.

One of the most heavenly modulations comes in the measure before the repeat of "O, Bächlein meiner Liebe" (O, dear brook). The agogic way of hitting the B major chord has the effect of a faint sigh.

In number seven, "Ungeduld" (Impatience), the young man's love rages on at full speed. The introduction, when played with meticulous attention to the accents, rests, and staccato markings, gives the whole idea of impatience, an effect that will be lost completely if it is played too fast. The tempo indication says *etwas geschwind* (*somewhat* fast, only).

The singer has to express many different images: words of love written in the bark of a tree, chiseled in stone, and sown with the fast-growing cress. The audience should be able to picture the young man sighing them into the morning breezes; the fragrance of flowers will carry them along to the girl. This excitement and

(Suggested MM: ♩=44)
Ja, heisst das ei - ne Wört - chen, das an-dre hei-sset
p
nein, die bei - den Wört-chen schlie - ssen die gan- ze Welt mir
cresc.
p
p
ein. die bei - den Wört-chen schlie-ssen die gan- ze Welt mir
cresc.
ein. O Bäch - lein mein-er Lie - be,
pp

impatience must be maintained through all four verses and should not be stopped by hanging on to high notes or making misunderstood ritardandi on the last phrases (suggested MM: ♩=116).

The serenade "Morgengruss" (Morning Greeting), though charming and seductive, has no such effect on the girl, who turns her face away. The young miller implores her to let his love take away all suffering and sorrow from her heart. The performer must try to express astonishment and a naïve lack of understanding. The "fool in love" does not suspect she does not love him in return (suggested MM: ♩=66).

Number nine, "Des Müllers Blumen" (The Miller's Flowers), describes flowers that are the same color as her eyes. Therefore, he believes, they belong to him. Even in her dreams, he says, the flowers should whisper to her, "Forget me not." I suggest that the third verse be sung almost in a whisper. In that way you will obtain a fine contrast with the *mezzo forte* of the fourth verse, describing her lively waking up and opening of the shutters (suggested MM: ♩.=52).

"Tränenregen" (Rain of Tears) gives a detailed description of the two sitting on the bank of the brook, gazing into the water. Sky and clouds, flowers and stars, are reflected in the brook's surface. The boy's heart is so full that a tear drops from his eye. The silly girl wants to go home because she thinks the falling tear is rain. Or does she use it only as an excuse? In the fourth verse, Schubert uses one of his ingenious modulations, this time from major to minor, to suggest that the denouement is drawing closer. Only the girl's last prosaic words are again in the major key (suggested MM: ♩.=44).

In "Mein!" (Mine), as if suspicions or disappointments had never existed, the boy explodes with an enthusiastic "She is mine!" Schubert indicates *mässig geschwind* (moderately fast); therefore, feel two beats to the measure, not four. Love has its ups and downs, and the miller's exuberant and sanguine mood almost foreshadows the growing doubts of the next song. Though this is one of the technically more difficult songs of the cycle, the singer must do his utmost to convey the character of improvisation by giving the impression that the exclamations just occurred to him. "Brook, stop your murmuring, mill wheels, leave your mumbling, birds, stop your singing so that my word 'mine' is the only one that can be heard." Otherwise it may easily sound contrived.

Though it is not indicated, I suggest that you feel two beats to the measure. In all the phrases, the accent of the musical line definitely divides every measure in two and gives the song the needed lightness.

Number twelve, "Pause" (Pause), is rich in musical inventions and is a challenge to any performer. Compared with the simplicity of "Das Wandern," it indicates the high development of Schubert's compositional genius. In many respects it foreshadows the more complex songs of *Winterreise*—"Rast," for example, or "Letzte Hoffnung."

The interpreter has to change incessantly from sentimental, sustained phrasing to impatient despair in jerking, sobbing outbursts.

There are two questions at the end of the song; the first one, in minor, should be expressed in a sad, dark tone of voice; the second one, in major, should be done hopefully, as with a great deal of wishful thinking. Is it an echo of my sufferings I hear when the green ribbon touches the strings of my lute? Or is it a prelude of new songs? An intermission could come at this point in the cycle.

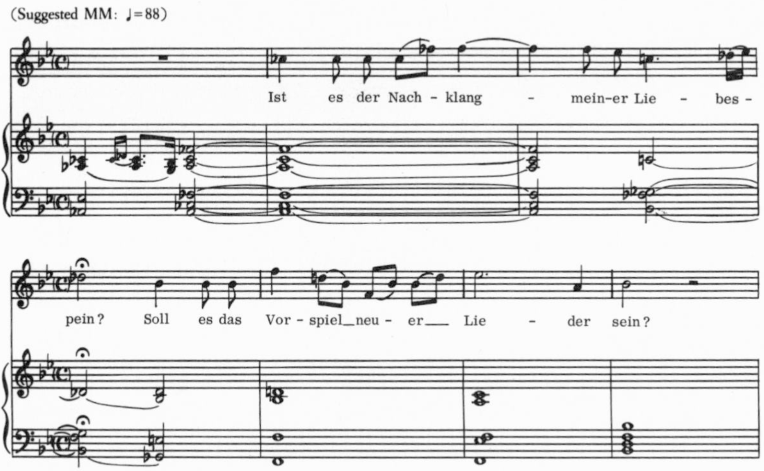

In "Mit dem grünen Lautenbande" (With the Lute's Green Ribbon), the girl thinks it is a pity that the lute's green ribbon is losing its color as it hangs on the wall. "All right," says the miller, "I will give it to you, and you can bind it round your hair, for you apparently like green. Oh, yes, green stands for hope and our love is evergreen. Or how?" In this musically simple song the skillful interpreter can portray the miller's naïveté and love and also the tension that is mounting as the denouement approaches. As he (and you) sing about the girl's preference for green, you must make it clear that the boy is trying to find every possible excuse for her. The shock of the bare truth will come anyway in the strong introduction to the next song (suggested MM: ♩=52).

In "Der Jäger" (The Huntsman), number fourteen, the truth

finally hits him. The music is sudden, fast, and staccato. Painfully, he now fully understands her coldness and reticence toward him. She does not love him, the *white* miller. She loves the *green* hunter! The two colors take on new meaning. The tempo indication is *Geschwind* (fast), but the miller's despair and anger are impossible to express if the words are sung too fast. In his desperate attempts to ridicule his rival, the miller uses such words as "trotziger" (obstinate or pigheaded), "struppige Haar" (your stiff bristles), and "Jägerheld" (proud hunter hero). Take your time. Stress these key words. Take advantage of the many German consonant clusters to create a reaction in the audience of shock and indignation (suggested MM: ♩. = 112).

In "Eifersucht und Stolz" (Jealousy and Pride), his jealousy produces a wild attack on her for being so fickle. He is proud, though, and asks the brook to tell her that he is fine. I suggest that you sing the opening phrases legato and leave the "tearing of the jealous heart" to the piano. This time you hear, not the peaceful

(Suggested MM: ♩= 126)
Wenn von dem Fang der Jä - ger lu - stig zieht nach Haus,
mf
da steckt kein sitt - sam Kind den Kopf zum Fen - ster 'naus,

bubbling of the brook, but a wild, turbulent, and furious creek in the accompaniment.

Later on, "Wenn von dem Fang der Jäger lustig zieht nach Haus" (When the huntsman comes home from the hunt), you should almost hammer out the separate words, while the horns in the accompaniment mock the jealous lover. Then return to a seemingly happy legato in "Er schnitzt bei mir sich eine Pfeif' aus Rohr, und bläst den Kindern schöne Tänz' und Lieder vor!" (He cuts a flute from a reed and blows beautiful dances and songs for the children).

The green color is dear to her, but hateful to him. In "Die liebe Farbe" (The Beloved Color), the first of the two "color" songs, he bewails the fact that she loves green. Yet, ironically, he wants to dress in green, hide himself in a green cypress grove, and be buried under the green grass, all because green is *her* favorite color.

It is difficult to sing two beats to a measure in this plaintive melody, but to avoid oversentimentality, give it some lightness. The second verse contains an appeal to himself to go hunting and should be sung *mezzo forte*. The third, with its premonition of death, should be done *pianissimo* (suggested MM: ♩=42).

"Die böse Farbe" (The Hateful Color), number seventeen, describes his desire to do anything to destroy the hated green, even to weeping until it becomes white. He wishes to lie down in despair before her door in wind, rain, and snow—and sing! The singer must convey the miller's derangement and make it believable to the listeners.

As in "Eifersucht und Stolz," all his fury and spite are directed against the girl more than against the hunter. Where the staccato phrases of the accompaniment indicate the tooting of the horn, the voice should be almost parlando, expressing the miller's white-hot rage. After his wild request to tear the green ribbon from her hair, he sings a last good-bye in long legato phrases and reveals that he still loves her. This should be sung warmly and caressingly (suggested MM: ♩=63).

In "Trock'ne Blumen" (Dry Flowers), he asks in sad resignation that the flowers she was false enough to give him be laid on his grave. Too late she will realize that he meant well. Everything is over.

The singer should use a small and almost dry voice to illustrate the still, sad picture of withered flowers dampened by tears. Watch the two beats to the measure. The simple theme was used by Schubert in a composition for flute and piano. The voice should be even and flutelike in order to come as close as possible to Schubert's own sound image. But when the miller wants the flowers to greet her at the end of the song, the singer can use full voice to try to express his last wish (suggested MM: ♩=40).

"Der Müller und der Bach" (The Miller and the Brook) is a moving dialogue between the mortally depressed miller and his friend, the brook. The brook tries to comfort the boy, telling him that a new star is born whenever true love fights its way through sorrow: but in vain. The brook does not know what love sometimes does to a young man.

Here you must contrast the miller's mood and the brook's mood, but as he always does, Schubert helps you along in your interpretation. The sad mood of the miller's phrases are in minor and the accompaniment stems the flow of the melody; the phrases of the brook are in major and move along briskly in an attempt to dispel the melancholy of the miller.

But to no avail. The singer *and* the miller prepare for the final song in a mild request to the brook, "Liebes Bächlein, so singe nur zu!" (Dear brook, sing on) (suggested MM: ♪=84).

In "Des Baches Wiegenlied" (The Brook's Lullaby), the brook in which he drowned himself sings a most moving lullaby over him. The singer will obtain the rocking effect of a lullaby only if he clearly sings it in two, and not too slowly. There are five verses, and I suggest you sing the first two softly, the next two louder, and verse five *pianissimo* to end the cycle as softly as possible (suggested MM: 𝅗𝅥=40).

Never allow yourself to be so moved by the sadness of the story that you almost cry. If you do, the catastrophe may happen; you may get a lump in your throat and be unable to sing. You must give the illusion that you are objective or removed from all the emotion. (Listen to Aksel Schiøtz and Gerald Moore. I am so presumptuous as to recommend my own recording in order to demonstrate most clearly how I still think *Die schöne Müllerin* should be interpreted, even though the recording of these songs was made in 1945.)

Not until the singer feels that he knows something about the sufferings of life should he dare tackle the interpretation of Schubert's other great cycle, *Winterreise*. While *Die schöne Müllerin* is about a youth whose happy love is suddenly changed into disappointment and despair, this cycle concerns a young man whose beloved has deserted him even before the cycle opens. The twenty-four songs are twenty-four different aspects of despair and sorrow, and it takes a mature interpreter to do justice to all these variations of dark moods.

The twenty songs of *Die schöne Müllerin* occupied a great part of my musical life when I started as a professional singer. It was not until I had experienced events of the most different kinds—such as my difficult decision whether to become a teacher or a singer, the Nazi occupation of Denmark, which closed the world to me, and serious surgery, which forced me to silence for a couple of years—that I finally performed the *Winterreise* cycle. These experiences proved to be of the greatest value to me when I tackled the songs. Without the maturity I gained through these bitter experiences, I doubt that I could have given truthful expressions to the wide range of desperate feelings of the jilted lover in *Winterreise.*

Disillusionment and sad resignation interspersed with short fits of bitter renunciation are some of the feelings you should convey to your listeners in "Gute Nacht" (Good Night), the first song in the cycle. To get an idea of the tempo, beat two; think of the jilted lover plodding along in the snow with a moonbeam as his only companion. This picture will help you understand the unreal and misty atmosphere surrounding the start of the journey. The desperate "Was soll ich länger weilen, dass man mich trieb' hinaus" (Why should I stay here any longer, since I was driven out) is marked *pianissimo,* which definitely must be a publisher's error. I suggest a slight *crescendo* in the accompaniment just before the vocal line enters. The impatience and bitterness of his outburst, "Why should I stay? Let the dogs bark their heads off," I would only be able to express *mezzo forte.*

In "Die Wetterfahne" (The Weather Vane), the loud start of the introduction that tapers out and leads into the soft beginning of the vocal line gives the listener the needed shock after the repressive mood of the first song.

The restlessness of the tempo when he accuses her of having

(Suggested MM: ♩=50)

chosen a rich bridegroom instead of himself gives an idea of the fickleness of her heart, which he compares to the weathercock on the roof of her house. The tempo indication is *Ziemlich geschwind* (somewhat fast); you will miss the *unruhig* (restless) effect of the weather vane if you do it very fast, which is tempting, I must admit (suggested MM: ♩.=69).

The tempo of "Gefror'ne Tränen" (Frozen Tears) is almost the same as in "Gute Nacht," as we continue the wanderings of the desperate lover. He wonders how his tears can freeze so quickly when they come from a glowing heart. Compare the "tear" theme of the introduction to that of "Tränenregen" from *Die schöne Müllerin.* There, overwhelming joy made the boy weep, but here, sheer sorrow and despair must be expressed.

In this song there is a classic example of how a performer of Schubert's songs should execute the appoggiatura. Max Friedländer comments in an excellent article: "it depends on the musical taste of the individual singer how to execute many of the more tricky examples of the appoggiatura."*

Number four, "Erstarrung" (Frozen Rigidity), contains the first sign of the young man's insanity, which is to reappear in some of the later songs of the cycle. How could he reasonably expect to find her footprints under the thick layer of snow that covers the

* Max Friedländer, ed., *Schubert,* albums I–VIII (usually included in vol. I) (New York: C. F. Peters Corporation).

(Suggested MM: 𝅗𝅥=54)
Ei Trä - nen, mei-ne Trä - nen,
pp

Ei Trä - nen, mei-ne Trä - nen,
pp

grass on which they once walked together? In his madness, he will try to penetrate the ice and the snow with his tears or with his kisses.

The accompaniment is very full, but basically it must be done *pianissimo*, as it is marked, or it will drown the vocal line. Schubert indicated that it be rendered *ziemlich schnell* (somewhat fast) only (suggested MM: ♩=160).

In "Der Lindenbaum" (The Linden Tree), sweet memories of dreams of love in the shade of the linden tree call him back to the dear place. But he does not look or listen, even though it was such a peaceful and happy time that he spent there. The first two verses and the last verse of the song have a folk song character about them. The singer should sing in a simple, straightforward manner. The accompaniment to the third verse, as in the prelude and the postlude, is difficult and is dreaded by all pianists, but it should be played and phrased so that you almost shiver in the cold wind.

The singer must try to characterize or accent the key words: "Die *kalten* Winde *bliesen* mir *grad* in's Angesicht, der Hut *flog* mir vom Kopfe, ich wendete mich *nicht*" (The cold wind blew right into my face, the hat flew off my head, I did not turn round). In the second half of the fourth verse, the almost haunting accom-

paniment is strengthened by octaves, and the voice should be somewhat restrained, as if disappearing while the linden tree continues its rustling.

In "Wasserflut" (Flood), we have teardrops in the snow again. The snow melts and is carried away by the brook, but his tears are warm when the water runs past her house. Schubert writes triplets against sixteenth notes and thereby obtains the jerky effect of sobbing. I don't agree at all with the theory that it should be done as triplets both on the piano and in the voice. It should be *langsam* (slow) but not *sehr langsam* (very slow).

Man - che Trän aus mei - nen Au - gen ist ge-fal - len in — den Schnee:
pp

Frozen, silent, and motionless lies the river in "Auf dem Flusse" (On the River). In the ice that covers the stream he writes her name and the day and the hour he first met her. The feelings still fill his heart, even if they have become as lifeless and silent as the frozen water. You have to express two sentiments—cold, frozen despair, and still-smoldering love—switching from one to the other constantly (suggested MM: ♩=46).

In number eight, "Rückblick" (A Backward Glance) (suggested MM: ♩=104), the restlessness of the lover trying to run away from *her* town with all its memories, good and bad, is expressed in the syncopated and stumbling rhythm between the right and left hands of the accompanist. A *crescendo* in the first measure followed by a *sforzando* on the first beat of the second create the wild character of the song. The middle part should be done very legato, but not necessarily slower.

The song ends as it begins. In spite of all, he would go back and stand still in front of her house (compare "Der Doppelgänger"). Even if there is no ritardando marked, I suggest the last "vor ihrem Hause stille stehn" (before her house stand still) be slightly more tenuto than the first. Schubert warns in his tempo indication: *Nicht zu geschwind!* (Not too fast).

"Irrlicht" (Will-o'-the-Wisp) (suggested MM: ♩=56), with its big intervals and wide range, is one of the most difficult songs, musically speaking. Jumps, dotted notes, and runs of thirty-second notes should be done as legato as possible. Interpreting this song is not too difficult though. The jilted lover says "Wie ich einen Ausgang finde, liegt nicht schwer mir in dem Sinn" (I am not concerned about finding a way out). Resignation is the prevailing mood; therefore, I suggest a dark shade of voice all the way through. Being misled is a familiar feeling to the young man; all his sufferings will eventually lead to the grave, anyway.

Generally, a song starts where the introduction starts. But, for once, the introduction to "Rast" (Rest), number ten (suggested MM: 𝅗𝅥=48), stands alone and ends with a fermata. Schubert intended a "full stop" after the very expressive piano introduction to the song. Then follows the song. As long as the unhappy lover keeps wandering along, life is tolerable; but the moment he stops, he almost gives up. His sufferings increase in the stillness. The singer must give the illusion of an exhausted and depressed human being who can't face the world any more and who wants only rest and resignation.

In "Frühlingstraum" (Spring Dream), the jilted lover has a dream. The unreal nature of all the beautiful things he sees and hears in the dream is described in the first part of this song, which should be sung in a soft and veiled way. Cruel reality is described in the middle part of the song, which should be sung in close

(Suggested MM: ♩. = 56)

Ich träum- te von bun - ten Blu - men, so wie sie wohl blü - hen im Mai,
p

to double tempo, as indicated. The mood is one of agitation, as shown in the jerky and frightening character of the accompaniment.

(Suggested MM: ♩. = 100)

Schnell
Und als die Häh - ne kräh-ten, da ward mein Au - ge wach;
3
3
mf
f
p
f

The conclusion in the third part of the second verse asks, "Wann grünt ihr Blätter am Fenster? Wann halt ich mein Liebchen im Arm?" (When do you frost leaves on the window pane turn green? When do I hold my love in my arms?) Never. This should be the hopeless undercurrent of the whole song. There is nothing happy and gay about it, though it is often performed this way. Remember that the seemingly joyous first part is only a dream.

In "Einsamkeit" (Loneliness)—as in numbers one, three, six, and ten—we have another description of the poor lover plodding sadly along. Giving different expressions to the same state of mind is not easy. One way to avoid the possible monotony is to stress

(Suggested MM: ♪=66)

the key words: "trübe" (dismal), "mattes" (feeble), "trägem" (dragging), and most important of all, "einsam" (lonely). The passionate outburst, "Ach, dass die Luft so ruhig, ach, dass die Welt so licht!" (Oh, that the air should be so calm, oh, that the world should be so bright!), is very exciting, as is the phrase, "Als noch die Stürme tobten" (When the storms still raged), with its furious repeated triplets ending on an abrupt *sforzando* chord.

(Suggested MM: ♩=44)

One of the most beautiful yet simple phrases of this song occurs in the accompaniment. It should be performed with all the soloistic expression the pianist can muster. It serves as an introduction to the line, "War ich so elend nicht" (I was not so wretched as this.)

The gripping effect of the first twelve songs of *Winterreise*, on the listeners as well as the performer, is by now so intense that a break is almost imperative. Most authorities agree that this is the natural place to put an intermission. That Schubert composed these songs in two rounds is, to me, evidence enough to support this.

The horn that opens "Die Post" (The Post) and the second half of the program is the one and only happy note in the whole cycle. It is a ray of hope, but it does not last. The lover's feeling of disappointment when the mailman has no letter for him puts an end to his hope.

John Newmark, the outstanding pianist from Montreal, once accompanied me in *Winterreise*. "Often," he said, "you will hear

(Suggested MM: ♩.=88)

this song done much too fast, as if it were a jet plane carrying the mail. An old mail coach, drawn by four horses up and down through the Austrian hills, only moves *etwas geschwind* (somewhat fast). Imagine the postillion bobbing happily up and down on the horse he is riding: There is your tempo!"

You don't have to slow down in the second half of the melody. The change from the dotted riding rhythm to the quieter quarter- and eighth-note tune will take care of that.

The singer must make a clear distinction between the half step in the twelfth measure from the end and the whole step in the eighth measure from the end. Attention to this fine point makes the phrases more fervent and urgent.

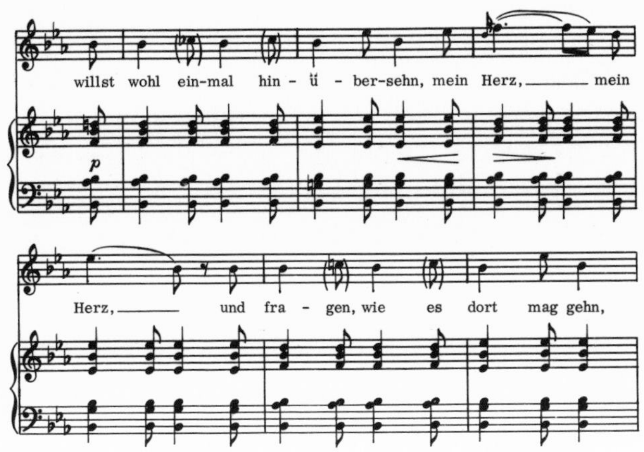

The song is addressed to the lover's own heart, and the phrase "Mein Herz" should be varied as much as possible. Don't sing it *fortissimo* all eighteen times.

In "Der greise Kopf" (The Hoary Head), number fourteen (suggested MM: ♩=56), the winter wanderer morbidly rejoices that his hair is tinged with white, showing that he has grown old.

But it is only hoarfrost; he is still a young man with many miserable years lying ahead. In spite of all his troubles, he did not grow white-haired overnight.

A simple expressive scale in the accompaniment leads into the key phrase, "wie weit noch bis zur Bahre" (how far yet to the death-bier). (Compare "war ich so elend nicht" in number twelve, "Einsamkeit.")

In "Die Krähe" (The Crow) (suggested MM: ♩=42), the description of the crow (not the *raven,* as it is often translated) circling above the head of the wanderer, waiting for him to drop dead from exhaustion, adds to the eeriness of this somber cycle.

The fluttering movement in the accompaniment will not be discernible if the song is sung, as it frequently is, in a slow tempo. Also, the phrase "Eine Krähe war mit mir aus der Stadt gezogen" (A crow followed me out of the town), and the following one, "ist bis heute für und für um mein Haupt geflogen" (has all the time been circling round my head), as well as the last, "Krähe, lass mich endlich seh'n Treue bis zum Grabe" (Crow, do let me see, at last, faithfulness unto death), should be sung in one breath. This is next to impossible in a slow tempo.

The fluttering of the last leaf on the tree to which he has attached his hope is ingeniously described in the introduction to number sixteen, "Letzte Hoffnung" (Last Hope). It is difficult to express simultaneously both the fluttering leaf and the lover's despair as his hope dies when the leaf falls to the ground.

The opening seems almost modernistic, with its surprising rhythms and intervals, and the phrase "Ach, und fällt das Blatt zu Boden" (Oh, when the leaf falls to the ground) with its syncopated, descending scale.

Then, again, we have one of those simple and beautiful phrases for which Schubert is so famous: "Wein, wein" (Weep, weep).

wein, wein auf mei - ner Hoff - nung Grab,
p

If you begin in a relatively slow tempo, it is easier to keep the same speed all through the song.

There are in this cycle many tone paintings and imitations of sounds done in an exquisite and poetic way, not just realistically and mechanically. One of the truest is in the introduction and accompaniment to "Im Dorfe" (In the Village). When dogs sleep, they often growl and bark softly in their dreams. This is exactly what is happening in the piano in the opening bars. The accompaniment starts *pianissimo* with an accent on the barking, grows louder, and then fades away. The voice sings "Es bellen die Hunde" (The dogs are barking) so softly that you can hear the dogs bark in the distance. People dream, too, about the good things that are in store for them. "Go ahead barking, you dogs. I see no reason why I should sleep or dream any more."

In "Auf dem Flusse," the jilted lover compared his heart to the raging water of the river, now covered with ice. In "Der stürmische Morgen" (Stormy Morning), number eighteen (suggested MM: ♩=96), his turbulent, confused feelings are likened to torn and

(Suggested MM: ♩.=66)

rugged clouds. "Und rote Feuerflammen zieh'n zwischen ihnen hin" (Red flames move between them). It is an excellent picture of the desperate state of his heart.

In staccato and jerky rhythms, this outburst of miserable despair is the most violent, difficult music in the whole cycle. The performers, both singer and accompanist, must try to check and control the wild music by not going too fast.

In number nine, "Irrlicht," he felt his wanderings to be aimless. In number nineteen, "Täuschung" (Delusion) (suggested MM: ♩.=66), he gladly follows the enticing light that makes him believe he is moving toward a warm house in which lives a dear soul. But it is all illusion, and the performer must try to convey this.

Sing "Der Wegweiser" (The Signpost) in the same "plodding" mood and tempo used in so many previous songs. The wanderer avoids people and the trodden path. He wants to hide from the world, and there is one signpost that points toward a place from which no one returns.

The phrases "Habe ja doch nichts begangen, dass ich Menschen sollte scheu'n" (I have done nothing so wrong that I should shy away from people) and "Einen Weiser seh' ich stehen, unverrückt vor meinem Blick" (I see a signpost stand immovably before me)

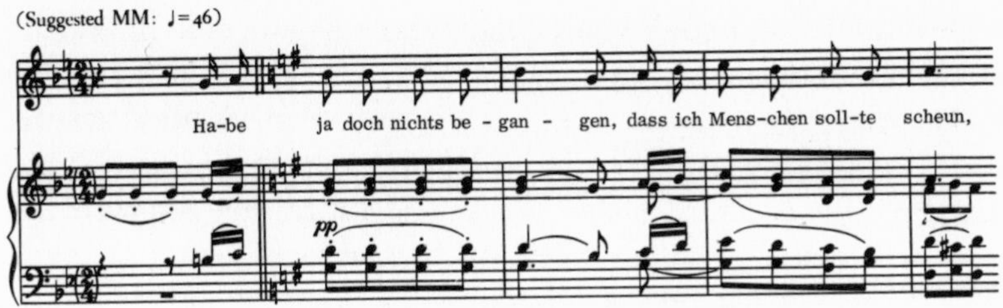
(Suggested MM: ♩=46)
Ha-be ja doch nichts be - gan - gen, dass ich Mens-chen soll-te scheun,
pp

could hardly be simpler; yet they are so beautiful, and the singer should emphasize them, even if all the harmonic changes take place in the piano part.

Note the ascending scale in the bass of the accompaniment on the repeat of the "einen Weiser" phrase. If you let this line stand out in a *crescendo* from *pianissimo* to *forte,* the effect will be tremendous.

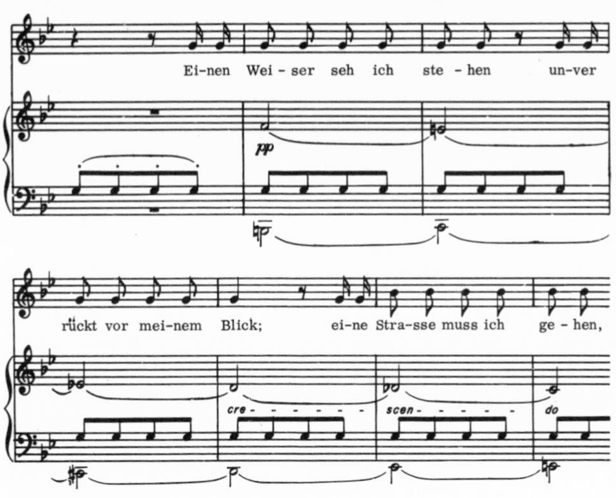
Ei-nen Wei - ser seh ich ste - hen un-ver
pp
rückt vor mei-nem Blick; ei-ne Stra-sse muss ich ge - hen,
cre - - - - - - scen - - - - - do

As always in Schubert's songs, the closer you adhere to his indications, both dynamically and rhythmically, the better the result.

There are no religious thoughts whatsoever in number twenty-one, "Das Wirtshaus" (The Inn), but the solemn character of the hymnlike introduction and indeed of the entire song supports the idea that there should be something unearthly in your interpretation. Convey a message of beauty by the solemnity of your tone and the intensity of your expression. The liberation that death would bring, but that is denied to the restless wanderer, is a familiar thought in the midst of all his misery (compare number fourteen, "Der greise Kopf").

The repetition of the first theme in the piano interlude adds to the calm and steady pace of the song (and thereby helps the singer

in his efforts), especially if the two eighth-note pickups are played strictly in the *sehr langsam* tempo that Schubert has indicated.

The key word is "unbarmherz'ge" (merciless) in the last stanza, and it should be stressed, of course.

An almost atheistic defiance and anger against God is the message of "Mut" (Courage). The wild, violent introduction is marked *forte* and "sets the scene" for the song.

In order to express the contrast of the beginning four lines of the first two verses, it is a good idea to change from *mezzo forte* to *forte*.

mf: *Fliegt der Schnee mir ins Gesicht*
(If the snow flies into my face)

f: *schüttl' ich ihn herunter,*
(I shake it off,)

mf: *Wenn mein Herz im Busen spricht*
(When my heart speaks in my bosom)

f: *sing' ich hell und munter.*
(I sing brightly and merrily.)

"Lustig" in the last verse means "gay," but there is nothing happy about this song. There is only irony, bitterness, and spite. Notice that all interludes or piano solo phrases are marked *forte*.

In "Die Nebensonnen" (The Mock Suns) (suggested MM: ♩=46), the poet has chosen the meteorological phenomenon of the appearance of two reflected suns, one on either side of the real sun, as the basis of his poetic idea. The "mock" suns are his love's two eyes, which now belong to someone else, and the unhappy lover would be much better off if the third sun, the real one, went down and everything became dark.

The melodic line is centered around the same note with only a few small modulations. The last sobbing cry of despair is somewhat subdued and serene. Sing with an unreal veiled tone, as if the grieving lover were seeing the suns through tears.

It was a stroke of genius to end this cycle with "Der Leiermann"

(Suggested MM: ♩=104)

Ziemlich geschwind, kräftig
f
(mf)
Fliegt der Schnee mir ins Ge - sicht,
(f)
schüttl ich ihn her -
p
un - ter.
(mf)
Wenn mein Herz
p
im Bu-sen spricht,
(f)
sing ich hell und mun - ter;
f

(The Hurdy-Gurdy Man) (suggested MM: ♩=56), an almost static picture of the old organ grinder. Nothing is more miserable and bleak than the description of the old man walking barefoot back and forth on the ice. Nobody listens to his playing; the dogs growl at him.

Many a singer is tempted to "do something" with this very simple song. But it is just its monotony that produces the effect of frozen stillness and complete hopelessness that Schubert no doubt intended. "Und er lässt es gehen alles wie es will" (And he lets everything come as it happens) is the key phrase.

In the last two lines, the wanderer turns to the old man and asks him to accompany his songs on the organ. Here there should be a definite change in the voice and in the whole attitude of the performer; from hopeless resignation to desperate appeal. He must sound as if the old man were right there.

Schubert describes the organ grinder in somber and desolate colors; his hopelessness, resignation, and bleakness are matched by the despair in the jilted lover's soul.

Sometimes you hear the last line sung very loudly. But that would indicate a false ray of hope. Questions should most frequently be sung *piano,* as if the asker is already listening to the answer. Here no answer follows. (Listen to Dietrich Fischer-Dieskau and Hermann Prey.)

ROBERT SCHUMANN (1810–1856)

From Heine's collection of poems *Lyrisches Intermezzo* (Lyrical Intermezzo), Schumann chose sixteen poems and formed his *Dichterliebe* (Poet's Love) cycle around them. Schumann gives much more detailed indications of how he wants his music performed than Schubert does. One would think that the performer would find it easier, but for some reason, I, at least, find the interpretation of Schubert's songs more obvious and closer to my own artistic mentality. It took me quite some time to penetrate the subtleties of the *Dichterliebe* cycle. Now it has become a standard part of my repertoire.

Schumann's deep understanding of and sympathy with the thoughts and emotions in Heine's poetry are stunning. Only in some of Hugo Wolf's Mörike and Goethe settings will you meet a similar harmony of poetic feeling between words and music.

There is a closer musical connection between the separate songs of *Dichterliebe* than between those in Schubert's two cycles. Therefore, there should be almost no pause between the songs. To some extent the break depends on the character of the preceding song.

The first five songs form a unity of lyrical feeling that would be wrong to break. They are intense love songs, but by the fourth song, "Wenn ich in deine Augen seh" (When I look into your eyes), the singer must make it clear that he is singing about unhappy love: "Doch wenn du sprichst: ich liebe dich! so muss ich weinen bitterlich" (but when you say: I love you, then I must cry bitterly). The minor third of the phrase gives it a plaintiveness that is emphasized by the ritardando prescribed by Schumann. The happy major sixth that begins Beethoven's "Ich liebe dich" or Grieg's "Jeg elsker dig" (I love you), with its exuberant outbursts, are declarations of happy love and are in sharp contrast to Schumann's sad and deceptive "Ich liebe dich."

(Suggested MM: ♩=52)
ritard
doch wenn du sprichst: ich lie - be dich! so muss ich wei-nen bit - ter - lich.

(Suggested MM for the first songs: 1. ♩=42; 2. ♩=42; 3. ♩=92; 4. ♩=52; 5. ♩=50.)

There is an abrupt change to the dramatic baritone character of the next two songs, "Im Rhein, im heiligen Strome" (In the Rhine, in the holy stream) (suggested MM: 𝅗𝅥=63) and "Ich grolle nicht" (I bear thee no grudge) (suggested MM: 𝅗𝅥=44). In the first one the singer must give a vivid description of the structure of the cathedral, so admirably painted in the angular, jerky figure of the accompaniment. In the second part, "Im Dom da steht ein Bildnis" (In the cathedral there is a picture), both the singer and the accompanist must give the impression that they are listening to the organ playing *inside* the cathedral, and they must try to illustrate this in very legato phrasing. The third part of the song forms a sort of postlude, and the performers should convey the distinct picture of having left the church again. With the deep ring of the enormous bell in the accompaniment, the singer should again convey a feeling of listening.

The wild despair of "Ich grolle nicht" (the bitterness and resignation is the same expressed in "Die böse Farbe" of Schubert's *Die schöne Müllerin*) is brought out by overarticulating the German words "grolle," "Diamantenpracht" (diamondlike splendor), "Schlang' " (snake), and "elend" (miserable). "Grolle" is the key word. Even though the unhappy lover says "Ich grolle nicht" several times, the prevailing feeling of the song should be that in spite of this he *does* bear a grudge. In this way the irony of Heine's poem is made obvious.

The sudden transition to number eight, "Und wüssten's die Blumen" (And if the little flowers knew it) (suggested MM: ♩=54), from the violent dramatic to the mild lyrical expression, is one of the hardest in the cycle. Only when the singer has made all his preparations for the attack, both technically and mentally, may the pianist begin. The two must rehearse this many, many times.

Schumann was a pianist himself, and he created some very

complex accompaniments. "Das ist ein Flöten und Geigen" (There Is a Sound of Flutes and Fiddles) is one of the most difficult in the cycle, with its runs imitating flutes and violins in the right hand and trumpets blaring in the left. To add to the interpretational difficulties for both singer and pianist, he indicates a "not too fast" tempo. At the end of the second verse the rustic music of

the wedding procession becomes so loud that it threatens to drown the voice, which intentionally is marked *piano*. The true effect is obtained by putting a "sobbing" accent on "schluchzen" and "stöhnen" (sob and groan).

Number ten, "Hör' ich das Liedchen klingen" (When I Hear the Little Song Sound) could be a small piano solo in itself, to which a simple vocal line has been added.

The three melodic lines clearly stand out in the accompaniment,

da - zwi - schen schluch - zen und stöh -
nen die lieb - li - chen En - ge - lein.
f

(Suggested MM: ♩=42)

Langsam
p
p
Hör' ich das Lied - chen klin - gen,

though it is not easy to decide which one is the "little song she sang."

Number eleven, "Ein Jüngling liebt ein Mädchen" (A Young Man Loves a Girl) (suggested MM: ♩=104), is in the gay and robust mood of the German "Studentenkorps" singing and breaks the languid feeling of the cycle. In the end, however, the singer has to make it clear to his audience that it is the familiar sad story of unrequited love.

Heine tells this story in a few simple statements. It is up to the singer to make the poet's ideas clear to the audience in a tempo that is not too fast. I think it is in accordance with Schumann's meticulous indications to suggest an accelerando during the last nine bars.

Number twelve, "Am leuchtenden Sommermorgen" (On a Bright Summer Morning) (suggested MM: ♩.=40), is another example of a song with a predominating piano part. Again and again we are reminded of the fact that Schumann was a pianist. This is a *Klavierstück* (piano piece). The singer has the privilege of fitting the vocal line to the beautiful patterns in the piano part.

Two "dream" songs follow: number thirteen, "Ich hab' im Traum geweinet" (I Wept in My Dreams) (suggested MM: ♩.=40), and number fourteen, "Allnächtlich im Traume seh' ich dich" (Every Night I See You in My Dreams) (suggested MM: ♩=54). It seems obvious to suggest a veiled sobbing voice throughout the first song with its staccato chords and the legato imitations of the vocal phrase before the third stanza.

The performer must attempt to create the unreal atmosphere of a dream in both these songs. To avoid the monotony of the sad heart-throbbing of "Ich hab' im Traum geweinet," I suggest a slightly brighter tone of voice in "Allnächtlich im Traume." As in Schubert's "Frühlingstraum" (Spring Dream), the young man is singing about a happy dream. It is only when he wakes to bitter reality that he has forgotten everything that might have soothed his misery.

In number fifteen, "Aus alten Märchen winkt es" (It Calls from

Old Fairy Tales) (suggested MM: ♩. = 100), the poet wishes he could return to the wonderful "never-never land" that he describes, but everything disappears as the mists fade in the rising sun. In number sixteen, the fanfarelike opening chords of "Die alten, bösen Lieder" (The Old, Bad Songs) express the poet's transfiguration. The singer needs all the intensity and sad shadings of his voice to express the despair and passion of "Die alten, bösen Lieder" (suggested MM: ♩ = 92). With a sigh of bitter resignation, he wishes to forget them and bury them. To the fairy-tale vision of the huge coffin being carried away by twelve giants, the singer must give life, not with gestures, but by stressing the key words—"bösen" (bad), "Träume" (dreams), "Sarg" (coffin), "Heidelberger Fass" (Heidelberg cask), "Riesen" (giants), "der starke Christoph" (the strong Christopher)—and by accenting the heavy steps of the funeral march in his singing.

At the end of this song the singer asks a question of his listeners—"Wisst ihr warum der Sarg wohl so gross und schwer mag sein?" (Do you know why the coffin has to be that big and heavy?)—and then gives the answer—"Ich senkt' auch meine Liebe und meinen Schmerz hinein" (I drowned my love and my pain, too). The beautiful and expressive piano postlude recalls the mood of previous songs. It encompasses all the misery and poetic love of *Dichterliebe*. The singer should try to relive all the emotions he has been trying to express in these sixteen gems of song, and he should *stand still* while he listens, together with his audience, to the postlude (listen to Fritz Wunderlich).

The French poet Louis Charles Adelaide Chamisso de Boncourt changed his name to Adelbert von Chamisso, moved to Prussia, wrote in German, and composed the cycle of sentimental poems called *Frauenliebe und -leben* (Woman's Love and Life). Schumann's music enhanced these poems and raised them above their level; they are very popular with female singers, who realize that no man can take this cycle away from them.

The frantic and intoxicated love, all the excitement of being engaged, preparing for the wedding, the bliss of being married, the terrible shock of the husband's sudden death—all these emotions are admirably expressed in Schumann's music. The soprano or contralto (it can be either) who presents this cycle is warned to restrain her own personal feelings so as not to impinge upon expressions of what is going on in the woman's heart. If the singer does not restrain her emotions, it is almost unbearable to listen to the cycle.

As in the case with the far superior *Dichterliebe,* Schumann created some wonderful piano interludes and a postlude that evokes memories of happier days. Whether you bow your head, stand motionless, or use facial expressions to connote your feelings during these piano "solos" is immaterial, as long as you eliminate your own self and listen together with the audience to the piano (listen to Janet Baker).

Schumann was strongly attracted to the cycle idea and wrote several "Liederkreise" (song cycles). The best known is *Liederkreis,* Opus 39, which is based on twelve poems of the truly romantic Josef von Eichendorff. I think it is perfectly all right for the singer to do individual songs from this cycle, since the songs are not so closely related as in many of the other cycles and not all are of the same high caliber as "Intermezzo," "Waldesgespräch" (Forest Dialogue), "Mondnacht" (Moonnight), and "Wehmut" (Sadness). It is, however, a great satisfaction to perform the whole cycle (listen to Fischer-Dieskau).

In contrast to the *Liederkreis, Der arme Peter* (The Poor Peter), the three Heine poems that Schumann set to music, contain such a unity of mood that they are almost one song. The singer should identify himself with Peter. A male singer is preferable, but since the story is told mostly *about* Peter, the feelings that fill his soul may very well be expressed by a woman, especially since the narrative switches from Hans and Grete, the happy couple, to the miserable Peter and to the girls in the street watching him.

As in the ninth *Dichterliebe* song, "Das ist ein Flöten und Geigen," the singer must make his audience hear the sounds of the happy wedding at the same time that he expresses the despair of poor Peter. Peter is in the dancing hall, where he can *see* his beloved in the arms of his rival: "Und schauet betrübet auf beide" (and looks sadly at the two). Even as the accompaniment "dances" along, the singer must let his voice shift from happy to unhappy sounds to underline the contrast of moods (listen to Gérard Souzay and Bernard Kruysen).

In number two, Peter's hopeless despair will be best expressed by watching the frequent tempo changes (suggested basic MM: 𝅗𝅥=80). You will have to have a funeral march in mind when you sing number three (suggested MM: ♩=48).

It is a special treat for the singer to sing the musical poetry of

Heinrich Heine with its strong emotional content and original and expressive language. That Heine's own German words should be used (rather than a translation) is to me obvious. The sounds of the words themselves, as in "Die Lotosblume" (The Lotus Flower) (suggested MM: ♩=92), paint the whole scene or situation. The phrase, "Und ihm entschleiert sie *freundlich* ihr *frommes* Blumengesicht" (And to him she kindly unveils her pious flower face), is filled with verbal sounds that should be almost savored by the singer. "Sie duftet und weinet und zittert" (She is fragrant and weeps and trembles) gives a marvelous image of the lovesick lotus flower adoring the moon. Sing it as softly and brightly as the moonlit night you are describing; at the same time watch closely Schumann's indications.

JOHANNES BRAHMS (1833–1897)

Johannes Brahms had an intimate knowledge of the human voice and its expressive power, a knowledge gained through extensive contact with singers, both soloists and choirs.

The nature of the tone produced by the voice is one of continuous flowing movement away from the singer to the ears of the listener. This is what makes the long cantabile lines of Brahms's songs so delightful and challenging to do. Phrases like "und die einsame Träne rinnt" (And the lonely tear runs) from "Die Mainacht" (Maynight), poetry by Hölty, or "Denn reich zu tränen pflegt das Aug' der Liebe" (for the eye in love is often weeping) from "Die Kränze" (The Wreaths), poetry by Daumer, or "und ziehe selig mit durch ew'ge Räume" (and move blissfully through the eternal space) from "Feldeinsamkeit," poetry by Allmer, are all written so wonderfully for the voice as an instrument that the singer should actually be more concerned about forming a well-shaped and colored expressive tone than about articulating the words.

und die ein - sa - me Trä -
espress.
- ne rinnt.

Denn reich zu trä - nen pflegt das
dolce
Aug' der Lie - be.
col Ped.

When the contralto voice hovers above the *pianissimo* male choir in the *Alt-Rhapsodie,* the audience will inevitably feel a shiver of excitement.

Brahms had a rare sense of the characteristics and colors of the human voice.

When one compares the songs of Brahms to those of Schumann before him or Hugo Wolf after him, one realizes that Brahms's interest in the vocal line over and above the meaning of the words is the special quality that separates him from other Lieder composers. In many ways Brahms can be thought of as more musician than poet. But let me hurry to protest against the erroneous idea that Brahms did not care about the words. In phrases like "wandl' ich traurig von Busch zu Busch" (I wander sadly from bush to bush) from "Die Mainacht," poetry by Hölty, or "Wie sturmestot die Särge schlummerten" (Like dead from the storm the coffins slumbered) from "Auf dem Kirchhofe," by Liliencron, with its chorale-like theme, the sad emotion of the words is admirably expressed in the music.

Characteristic of Brahms's way of setting a poem to music is the inspiration he gets from a single word or phrase. He often creates an entire composition around such a word. A typical example is one of his early songs, "Der Schmied" (The Blacksmith), a setting of a poem by Uhland (suggested MM: 𝅗𝅥. = 52), which centers around the image of a blacksmith wielding his hammer over the anvil. One is tempted to say that the words were "put on" the music *after* it had been composed. I suggest that the performer imagine that *two* blacksmiths are swinging their hammers alternately, or it will be impossible to achieve the allegro tempo that Brahms prescribes. A sledge hammer is heavy.

There has been a tendency (German?) to oversentimentalize Brahms's songs and give them a rubato treatment, which is usually too slow. It is understandable that a singer may feel tempted to indulge in the long lines so inviting to vocal excess, but in my opinion the music gains in authority and greatness if it is performed just as Brahms indicated.

A melody like "Immer leiser wird mein Schlummer" (My Sleep Is Growing Lighter), a setting of a poem by Lingg (suggested MM: 𝅗𝅥 = 42), is marked *alla breve* and should be sung with a strong feeling of two beats to the measure. When the tempo is tightened, the long arabesques of the lines gain intensity and a streamlined quality without losing any of their beauty.

The collection of songs called *Romanzen aus Magelone* (Romances from Magelone) is not really a cycle. The poems, which are scattered through the novel *Die schöne Magelone* (The Fair Magelone) by Ludwig Tieck (1773–1853) have only a loose continuity.

In a presentation of them, many interpreters recite a few lines from the novel before each song in order to emphasize what continuity there is and in this way get closer to the song-cycle idea.

From this collection of songs, it is perfectly acceptable to choose individual ones. I would suggest a group of four, as most of them may seem somewhat lengthy, at least for non-Germans. Number one, "Keinen hat es noch gereut" (Nobody Yet Regretted) (suggested MM: 𝅗𝅥. = 104), with its powerful galloping theme, would be an excellent opener for such a group. Number three, "Sind es Schmerzen, sind es Freuden" (Is It Pain or Is It Joy) (suggested MM: ♩=76), has the character of a full piano solo from a sonata, and at the same time the piano is an "assisting instrument" supporting and supplementing the voice. I recommend including it. Number nine, "Ruhe, Süssliebchen" (Rest, Sweet Love) (suggested MM's: ♩. = 50 and ♩. = 84), in which the knight keeps watch over the fair one, has the long vocal phrases known from "Die Mainacht" brought into full relief over a fast-moving middle part. I would end the group with the lively number fourteen, "Wie froh und frisch" (How Glad and Gay) (suggested MM: ♩= 104).

The performer would have a continuing story to tell in these four songs—a story of the boisterous young rider successfully making his way through life; the lovesick longing of youth and the firm belief that the only happiness is to be close to Magelone; the young man keeping anxious watch over the sleeping Magelone, whom he finally wins; and his impatience to get home after all the turbulent confusion during his travels. All the poems are addressed to the fair Magelone, and the feelings of Peter, the young knight, can and should be expressed only by a male voice.

Vier ernste Gesänge, Brahms's last work, is a cycle of four songs with texts from the scriptures. They leave a deep impact on both singer and audience, if performed in a strict and monumental way. These songs are classical in the truest sense of the word.

A clear distinction must be made between the first three songs, whose words are from the Old Testament, and the fourth, whose words are St. Paul's. In rendering the stern and cold statement of the Old Testament prophet—that there is no difference in the fate of man or beast—the singer should achieve an objective, almost superhuman state of mind. And the outbursts "O, Tod, wie bitter bist du" (O, Death, how bitter are you) and "O, Tod, wie wohl tust du dem Dürftigen" (O, Death, how comforting you are to him who needs you) should be those, not of an unhappy man deploring his fate, but of an objective observer, the prophet. (The suggested MM's for the first three songs are: 1. ♩=60 and ♩=152; 2. ♩=72; 3. 𝅗𝅥.=44.)

(Suggested MM: ♩=100)

Andante con moto ed anima
Wenn ___ ich mit Men - schen = und mit
En - gels=zung-en ___ re - de-te, und hät - te der Lie - be nicht,

The happy optimism of the Christian's belief in eternal life is struck at once in the opening chords of the fourth song. Now everything centers around the word "Liebe" (the Biblical connotation of this word is "charity," meaning love of one's neighbor). The phrase "und hätte der Liebe nicht" (and did not have charity) appears three times. Here, I suggest a slight slowing up and a *piano* voice, to clarify the contrast between all the things he mentions being useless: having angels' tongues, moving mountains, supporting the poor, etc. The singer must express St. Paul's firm Christian belief and his strong feeling of victory over Death. Brahms's soaring lines will help him express this message of love (listen to Fischer-Dieskau).

HUGO WOLF (1860–1903)

The thoughts and emotions of the poem are the inner core of the art song, and their interpretation is the singer's first duty. Without a deep understanding of the words, the music, which was inspired by the words, cannot come to life. In his book on Hugo Wolf, Frank Walker writes:

> The musician stood at the service of the poet, offering the resources of his art to illuminate the words and recapture the emotions that had inspired them. The peculiar resources that Wolf brought to this task included all he had learnt from a close study of his predecessors, Schubert and Schumann, together with an exhaustive . . . knowledge of the possibilities of verbal and emotional expression in music. The free declamatory methods of Wagner's operas applied to the miniature form of the song . . . made possible the full expression of complex sensations that had been beyond the reach of earlier masters of the Lied.*

* *Hugo Wolf: A Biography* (New York: Alfred A. Knopf, Inc., 1952).

In intertwining poetry and music, Hugo Wolf reached a perfection that his predecessors never attained or even imagined. From the titles of his various collections of songs it is obvious that Hugo Wolf matched his musical thinking to that of his poets. *Gedichte von Edward Mörike für eine Singstimme und Klavier von Hugo Wolf* (Poems by Edward Mörike for Voice and Piano by Hugo Wolf) is the title of his first song collection. This illustrates vividly how important the poem was for him.

I maintain that sometimes there are poems, e.g., by Michelangelo and Goethe, that are so demanding on the intellect that they should not be made into songs. Music should serve to elucidate, not to confound. In his excellent collection of German songs with English translations, Siegbert S. Prawer quotes Hegel, the German philosopher, as saying "the poem, made into a song, must not be too burdened with thought, too philosophical and deep,"* a view I heartily endorse.

To have the doors thrown open to the wonderful world of Hugo Wolf's songs is something of a revelation to the interpreter. I became intimately acquainted with Hugo Wolf only rather late in my career. Thus, I was offered a "chronological" advantage in my repertoire, because I was thoroughly familiar with Schubert, Schumann, and Brahms before I discovered the more complex treasures of Wolf. This proved to be of the greatest benefit for my whole understanding of the problems of interpretation. Only when the student has built a solid foundation with a thorough knowledge of the classical composers is he ready for Hugo Wolf.

The interpreter is overwhelmed by the incredible diversity of moods he has to express in the songs of Hugo Wolf's Mörike poems. Although they were often composed at the rate of three or four per day, what a variety Wolf achieved. Fortunately, he facilitates the job of interpretation by indicating clearly and unambiguously what to do and how to do it.

* *The Penguin Book of Lieder* (Baltimore: Penguin Books, Inc., 1964).

The muffled, hollow emptiness of the first four slow and *pianissimo* measures of "Das verlassene Mägdlein"* (The Deserted Girl) gives the singer an indication of the disconsolate mood of the girl, who has to make a fire before daybreak. Only the jumping and crackling of the sparks break the stillness of the dawn.

A wan and expressionless tone of voice should be used when singing about the girl gazing into the fire. From *pianissimo* the voice very abruptly rises into a *forte* cry of despair and anger, when she recalls that last night she dreamt about her faithless lover.

Don't let her tears tempt you to sing sentimentally. Rather, go back to the sad and monotonous voice you used in the opening of the song. For the young singer who wishes to become familiar with the many-colored images of Wolf's songs, the simpleness of "Das verlassene Mägdlein" is an excellent one to begin with. The emotions of the Mörike poem are uncomplicated and primitive.

It takes a young man, or someone young at heart, to sing "Der Tambour" (The Drummer Boy) (suggested MM: ♩=100). Hugo Wolf indicates that the song be sung *im Marschtempo,* though there is nothing martial about it. To emphasize the humor and sad irony of the warrior's road to victory, you will have to use a slow, stodgy tempo. I have always had an image of the soldiers of the Thirty Years' War or the ones in Bertolt Brecht's play *Mother Courage. They* marched rather slowly.

Also, you have to express the boy's emotions: his longing for his mother and her good cooking and his sentimental and wishful thoughts of his young fiancée, which the moonlight evokes in him.

This song requires an accomplished accompanist. Hugo Wolf never makes it easy for the accompanist. Yet the lines of the voice and piano cannot be separated. Throughout each individual song, we find seven or eight different patterns in the accompaniment, all dictated by the words of the poem. The interpreter is being greatly supported.

* *Mörike Lieder,* Vol. 1, No. 7 (New York: C. F. Peters Corporation, No. 8961).

(Suggested MM: ♪=72)

In "Schlafendes Jesuskind"* (The Christ Child Asleep), in order to bring across the idea of the sleeping child and the pervasive holiness of the scene, the whole song should be sung *piano, pianissimo,* or even *pianissisimo.*

I have never been able to understand how a pianist could play any softer than *pianissimo,* but this sort of indication must, of

* *Mörike Lieder,* Vol. 3, No. 1 (New York: C. F. Peters Corporation, No. 8990).

course, be taken in relation to what has preceded. (On many occasions Verdi even calls for a *diminuendo* following a *ppppp*!) In "Schlafendes Jesuskind," remember that you still have the *crescendi* and fervent climaxes in the song.

Frequently the vocal line is continued in the piano, and sometimes the other way around, so the singer must watch carefully that his vocal phrases never break the continuity.

Hugo Wolf's ingenious use of a syncopated rhythm when he needs an accent on certain words is very characteristic of his writing and greatly helps the musical interpretation. Triplet figures always indicate something hesitant, and their calm effect (they appear six times during the melody) is ingenious and should be meticulously observed.

Exuberant joy and dancing lightness is the setting of the scene that introduces one of Wolf's most boisterous and yet lyrically moving songs, "Auf einer Wanderung"* (On a Journey). The wanderer is enchanted by the idyllic charm of the little town through which he is passing. Suddenly he hears singing and is almost overwhelmed by the beauty of the scene. The interpreter must do his utmost to make his voice sound like bells and nightingales, so that not only the blossoms and the air and the roses are carried away, but the audience as well, even throughout the long

ecstatic interludes. In the climactic "O, Muse, du hast mein Herz berührt mit einem Liebeshauch!" (Oh, Muse, you touched my heart with a breath of love), you must summon up all the beauty your voice can produce in *fortissimo,* and then suggest the wanderer's

* *Mörike Lieder,* Vol. 2, No. 15 (New York: C. F. Peters Corporation, No. 8963), 14–19.

long, calm, and happy sweetness in the *diminuendo* of the last phrase. A long, wonderful postlude allows both singer and audience to relive the whole song.

Hugo Wolf was enamored of words and knew how to build his music not only to support them but also to unfold them in all their poetic beauty. "Blumenflor" (wealth of flowers), "Nachtigallenchor" (choir of nightingales), "Erlenbach" (willow branch), "Mühle" (mill), "Muse" (muse), and "Liebeshauch" (breath of love) are some of the words he uses that give the singer ample opportunity to let his audience participate in the sheer joy of good enunciation.

In "Fussreise" (A Country Walk) (suggested MM: ♩=132), the minister (Mörike himself) expresses a different kind of joy in his wanderings. You must set a comfortable pace from the beginning in order to prepare the audience for something calm and easy, not excitement, drama, or unhappy love. All nature rejoices in the work of the Creator, and he, also, is grateful: "Wie an ewig neuen Schöpfungstagen" (As in the eternally young days of Creation). He wishes that his life were as enjoyable and peaceful as his walk with his *Wanderstab* (walking stick).

In "Anakreons Grab"* (Anacreon's Grave), Hugo Wolf understood how to bring forth all the beauty and simplicity of this Goethe poem. The singer should accentuate the vowel sounds in the first two lines and the consonant clusters in the next two:

Wo die Rose hier blüht
(Here where the rose blooms)

Wo Reben um Lorbeer sich schlingen
(Where vines twine around laurels)

Wo das Turtelchen lockt
(Where the turtledove calls)

Wo sich das Grillchen ergötzt.
(Where the cricket loves to be.)

* *Goethe Lieder* (New York: C. F. Peters Corporation).

(Suggested MM: ♪=100)
zart
Wo die Ro - se hier blüht, wo Re - ben um Lor-beer sich schlin-gen,
wo das Tur - tel-chen lockt, wo sich das Grill-chen er-götzt,
sehr zart

You must feel a distinct pulsation of twelve slow beats in the measure, for only then will you be able to evoke the complete stillness and peace of the grave.

The phrase "Das alle Götter mit Leben schön bepflanzt" (that all the gods have planted and adorned with life) *must* be sung in one breath. This decides the tempo of the song, which is *sehr langsam,* that is, as slowly as possible (suggested MM: ♪=100).

You must bring out the happiness of Anacreon's life in a happy and bright tone of voice and then use a darker shade when you sing about the grave, which protects him against all bitterness.

You will obtain one of the most striking of musical effects if you follow Wolf's ingenious and dynamic indications at "Es ist Anakreons Ruh!" (It is Anacreon's resting place).

Hugo Wolf's songs, with their stunning variety, are a fruitful proving ground for the interpreter who wants to meet the challenge of the composer's thousand different musical expressions. A striking

contrast to the peace of "Anakreons Grab" is the Italian lyric about the "warm and willing" Carmenlike woman in "Ich hab' in Penna einen Liebsten wohnen" (In Penna Lives One of My Lovers), whose fickleness and braggadocio remind one of Leporello's report of Don Giovanni, with so many mistresses there and so many there, but in Spain "mille e tre" (1,003). A very flexible voice, and mind, too, is needed for this song.

In "Ich hab' in Penna" (Hugo Wolf's MM: ♩=160), the singer has to express the long *crescendo* in the woman's feelings. From her first amorous statement, "I have a lover in Penna," she works herself up to a victorious "and ten in Castiglione!" The audience must be brought to that climax, too, for only then does the long passionate postlude that Wolf marked *feurig* (with fire) make sense.

Wolf was a great admirer of Schubert, and only when he thought that there were ideas and emotions in a poem that had escaped Schubert's mind, did he reset the poem. "Kennst du das Land"* (Knowest Thou the Country), by Goethe, is a good example. Both Schubert's and Wolf's settings offer great challenges to the singer. Both are fine pieces of music, but because of Hugo Wolf's deeper insight into the poem, he has been able to get closer to the true concept of the various images in his musical expression than Schubert.

Take the openings of both settings:

* *Goethe Lieder,* Vol. 1, No. 9 (New York: C. F. Peters Corporation, No. 9110), 27.

Mässig
Kennst du das Land? wo die Ci-tro-nen blüh'n, im
p
3 3
dunk-len Laub die Gold-o-rang-en glüh'n,
Langsam und sehr ausdrucksvoll
p
p
Kennst du das Land, wo die Zi-tro-nen blühn,
hervortretend
pp
p sehr ausdrucksvoll
poco a poco cresc.
pp
im dunk-len Laub die Gold-o-rang-en glühn,
mf
p

My purpose in making this comparison is to show how close interpreter and composer can get to each other in Hugo Wolf's setting. Both are interpreters of the poem, but the performer will be a good one only if he walks in Hugo Wolf's footsteps, so to speak, and understands how to express all the longing and impatience that is so exquisitely evoked both in vocal phrases and in the syncopated rhythms of the piano part.

Among the wealth of poems set to music by Wolf with such unfaltering poetical understanding and musical taste is his "Herr, was trägt der Boden hier"* (Lord, What Does the Earth Carry), a short and concentrated dialogue between Christ and the soul. The anxious questions of the believer must be sung *piano* and almost timidly; and the answers of Christ dying on the cross, in a whispering, distant voice, but still with authority (listen to Fischer-Dieskau). "Dornen, liebes Herz, für mich, und für dich der Blumen Zier" (Thorns, dear heart, for me, and for you the beautiful flowers).

GUSTAV MAHLER (1860–1911) and RICHARD STRAUSS (1864–1949)

The songs of Mahler and Strauss offer great possibilities for the interpreter, but in my opinion they diverge from the Lied proper, most of them having been conceived as solos with orchestral accompaniment. Mahler wrote two song cycles: *Kindertotenlieder* (Songs on the Death of Children), which describes a father's inconsolable mourning for his children, who perished in a storm that he himself had sent them into, and *Lieder eines fahrenden Gesellen* (Songs of a Wayfarer), an exciting and beautiful presentation of the well-known theme of the young man whose beloved marries another (listen to Fischer-Dieskau).

There are great challenges for "operatic" voices in the Strauss songs "Befreit" (Freed), "Ständchen" (Serenade), "Cäcilie," "Zueignung" (Dedication), "Allerseelen" (All Souls' Day), and many others. In these, the vocal line is so sweeping and broad that a subtle interpretation of the poems is not essential. The effect

* *Spanisches Liederbuch* Geistliche Lieder No. 9.

of the brilliant voice with control and technique will make them come to life (listen to Schwarzkopf).

There can be no doubt about it: With the songs of Mahler and Strauss we have left the immaculate domain of the Lied.

FRENCH MÉLODIES

More than any other nation, the French have an almost sensuous love of their language. Their writers and poets are eager to have their works sound as refined and exquisite as possible, and they work closely with actors, *diseurs* or *diseuses*, and singers to that end.

The art of interpretation is highly developed in France. Claire Croiza, Régine Crespin, Charles Panzéra, Pierre Bernac, and Gérard Souzay, as well as the lighter artists, Yvette Guilbert, Edith Piaf, Maurice Chevalier, and Yves Montand are some of the great interpreters of the French *mélodies* or *chansons*.

Paul Valéry, the well-known French poet, found in the singing of Claire Croiza all the qualities he would have loved in the *diseuse* of his poems—an exquisite sense of rhythm, the accenting of essential words, the clear articulation of consonants, and above all, a deep understanding and a vivid imagination. In *Un Art de l'Interprétation,* Helen Abraham published notes she took while attending the master classes of Madame Croiza.* I want to quote some of her wise remarks on the singer's art in French songs.

"La première sagesse de l'interprète, c'est de connaître ses limites" (The first rule for an interpreter is to know his limitations). In other words, don't even try, if you are a man, to give the illusion that you are Lià, the mother who cries for her child, Azaël, in Debussy's cantata *L'Enfant Prodigue* (The Prodigal Son). Don't

* *Un Art de l'Interprétation* (Paris: Office de Centralisation d'Ouvrages, 1954).

try, if you are a woman, to interpret the lovesickness of Don Quichotte in Ravel's *Don Quichotte à Dulcinée.*

"Travailler les paroles en mesure, sans les chanter" (Practice reading the poem aloud before you sing it, but in measured time). This excellent piece of advice should be remembered in the preparation of any song you are going to perform. The rhythm, the heartbeat of the song, so musically essential, is the first thing to get into your system. Madame Croiza says about readiness: "Ne pas sauter sur l'expression comme sur un cheval qui passe!" (Don't jump on the expression as if it were a galloping horse!). Another great interpreter of French songs, Maggie Teyte, with whom I studied while she lived in New York, stressed the same idea. "Be ready!" she said, with a strong trill of her Scottish *r*.

The language of a nation reflects the character of its people and their way of expressing feelings and thoughts, and the differences in style between the German Lied and the French mélodie can be accounted for mainly by the differences in the German and French languages. For an English-speaking person, it seems to be easier to penetrate the German world of ideas than the French, perhaps because French is a Romance language and English and German are Germanic languages. Though English-speaking people may find the German language clumsy and awkward, French, with its many fine distinctions of pronunciation and the demands it makes for clear and precise enunciation, is something extremely "foreign" and may even seem affected to speakers of English, who often blur and swallow their words.

The German language is sometimes called "masculine" because of its use of strong consonant groups and chopped up words, as seen in Hugo Wolf's song "Fussreise." "Am frisch geschnitt'nen Wanderstab, wenn ich in der Frühe" (At the newly cut walking stick, when I wander in the morning). French, on the other hand, is sometimes called "feminine" because of its long, legato lines, as in Fauré's song from the cycle *La Bonne Chanson,* "J'allais par des chemins perfides douloureusement incertain" (I walked along treacherous paths painfully uncertain). This is perhaps even more obvious when comparing the French translation of the Heine poem that Schumann set to music in the *Dichterliebe* cycle:

Ich hab im Traum geweinet—
mir träumte, du lägest in Grab.
(I have wept in my dreams
I dreamt you lay in your grave.)

J'ai pleuré en rêve
j'ai rêvé que tu était morte.
(Music by George Hüe)

These examples clearly show the difference between the two languages. You almost have to force the German sentences to be lithe and supple in order to make a cantabile line, while in spoken French, it is already there.

A German word beginning with a vowel must be preceded by a slight glottal stop: "*I*ch wache *a*uf" (I wake up); "*A*uf *e*in *a*ltes Bild" (In an old picture). This tends to chop up the legato line. In a discussion of the characteristics of the language, Elisabeth Schwarzkopf once admitted that it actually would be easier to sing German if this stop were omitted, but she said, "if you made the sort of liaison you use in French, or for that matter in English, it just wouldn't be good German!" The French liaison produces a mellifluous, flowing effect, as in the following line from Fauré's "Chanson de Pêcheur": "Sous la tombe elle emporte mon âme et mes amours" [su la tɔ̃ bɛ‿·lã pɔrtəmɔ̃‿na me mɛ‿za‿mu:r] (She takes my soul and my love with her in the grave).

French singers are unsurpassed in their performance of the French song, though the Scotswomen Mary Garden and Maggie Teyte are exceptions to that rule. Non-French singers who attempt the many beautiful compositions of the French repertoire meet almost insurmountable difficulty creating the special "French" atmosphere. Listen to the intelligent and language-minded Dietrich

Allegro molto ♩= 152
p
J'ai pres-que peur, en vé - ri -
pp
té, Tant je sens ma vie en - la - cé - e.
mf

Munter
mf
Die Ro - se, die Li - lie, die Tau - be, die Son - ne, die liebt' ich einst al - le in
mf

Fischer-Dieskau's recording of *La Bonne Chanson,* and you will understand what I mean.

On the other hand, we find that French singers often run into serious trouble when they try to reproduce the style of the German and English song because it is difficult for them to disregard their own French concepts of tone production, diction, and phrasing. Charles Panzéra's German diction in his recording of *Dichterliebe* is an exception, but he is not "arch-French" but actually bilingual, having been born in Switzerland.

GABRIEL FAURÉ (1845–1924)

For the interpreter, Gabriel Fauré's song cycle *La Bonne Chanson* (The Good Song), consisting of nine poems by Paul Verlaine, offers possibilities similar to those encountered in *Dichterliebe.* With the same understanding of the intrinsic meaning and emotional content of the lyrics that Schumann had, Fauré created some of his greatest vocal compositions in this cycle. The singer rejoices in Fauré's genuine feeling for the possibilities of the voice in his supple phrasing of the lines and the fine nuances that he wants expressed.

Both in number five of *La Bonne Chanson,* "J'ai presque peur en vérité" (I Am Almost Afraid, Indeed), and in number three of *Dichterliebe,* "Die Rose, die Lilie, die Taube, die Sonne" (The Rose, the Lily, the Dove, the Sun), the singer must sustain a legato in his phrasing and leave the breathless, staccato character to the accompaniment. It is easier to do this in the French song because of the linear nature of the language.

From the interpreter's point of view, it is also interesting to compare Fauré with Hugo Wolf. Two widely different human feelings are exquisitely expressed by both composers in number six of *La Bonne Chanson,* "Avant que tu ne t'en ailles" (Before You Fade Away), and Wolf's "Das verlassene Mägdlein" (The Deserted Girl).

Quasi Adagio ♩=68
pp
A - vant que tu ne t'en ail - les pâle é -
toi - le du ma- tin.
pp

Langsam
pp
Früh, wann die Häh - ne krähn,
pp

etwas lebhafter

Plötz-lich, da kommt es mir, treu-lo - ser Kna - be,

f

f

In both songs there is a sudden contrast between gazing into the pale light of dawn before the stars fade away and then waking up to reality. Fauré expresses a feeling of infinite happiness: "Mille cailles chantent, chantent dans le thym" (Thousands of quail are singing in the thyme). Hugo Wolf expresses black despair: "Plötzlich da kommt es mir, treuloser Knabe" (Suddenly I realize, faithless boy).

Throughout *La Bonne Chanson,* the singer has to convey an ambiance of overwhelming happiness and love. I would recommend having a native Frenchman, preferably an actor or *diseur,* read the Verlaine poems aloud in your preparation for the performing of this cycle. When you hear all the shadings and inflections of the spoken language, you will realize how perfectly Fauré expressed the meaning of the poetry in his music, especially in "O, bien-aimée," from number three and "L'hiver a cessé," from number nine.

I had the great privilege of being coached in *La Bonne Chanson* by M. and Mme. Panzéra in 1953. My music is filled with the notes and comments that Fauré himself gave to Charles Panzéra when he studied the cycle with the composer. Madame Croiza comments: "On commence toujours les mélodies de Fauré trop triste. Chanter trop grave est la plus grande erreur." (Always the songs of Fauré are begun too sadly. To sing too seriously is the biggest error.) That certainly was not what I learned in the studio of Panzéra! Those were happy hours of understanding, poetic interpretation (listen to Panzéra and Gérard Souzay).

In another Verlaine poem, "Clair de Lune" (Moonlight), Fauré's music evokes the shimmering of the moonlit night, comparing all that happens in that unreal world to "her" soul. The voice should express the long legato lines independently of the minuet rhythm of Fauré's accompaniment. Even the lively and wide-ranged vocal line in "Mai" (Victor Hugo), must be sung as if the singer did not need to breathe at all. At any rate, his breathing must not be audible. Without any glissando or "scooping," one tone must merge im-

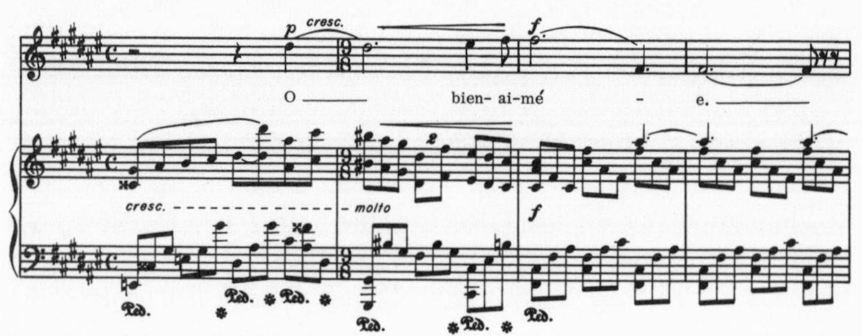
p cresc.
f
O
bien- ai-mé
- e.
cresc. molto
f
Ped.
Ped.
Ped.
Ped.
Ped.
Ped.

mf
f
L'hi - ver
a
ces -
f
p
sé
pp

perceptibly into the next: "Comme une lèvre au bas de la robe des cieux" (As a seam at the bottom of the dress of heaven).

HENRI DUPARC (1848–1933)

"L'Invitation au Voyage" (poetry by Charles Baudelaire), "Phydilé" (Leconte de Lisle), "Lamento" (Lament) (poetry by Théophile Gautier), and "Chanson triste" (A Sad Song) (poetry by Jean Lahor) are among the most popular songs of Duparc. Though Duparc wrote only about fifteen songs, to the interpreter they are all

very rewarding, for they give him an opportunity to express all the finesse and delicate shadings of French poetry.

Maggie Teyte is one of the most sensitive and electrifying performers I have ever heard. This is exemplified in her recording of "L'Invitation au Voyage." Notice her fine *crescendo* on "vivre ensemble" (live together). When she sings "Là, tout n'est qu'ordre et beauté, luxe, calme, et volupté" (There, everything is order and beauty, luxury, calm, and pleasure), she reaches one of the highest goals in the art of interpretation in her ability to put a tremendous expression on a seemingly insignificant word such as "là" and overwhelmingly so on important, expressive words like "luxe," "calme," and "volupté."

Leconte de Lisle's description of the warm and fragrant summer noon in "Phydilé" offers rich opportunities for the interpreter to paint and vitalize the lover's burning passion for Phydilé. The ac-

companiment will become more vivid when the words describe the buzzing bees, the splendor of the stars, her smile and her kisses, but the singer must sustain the beauty of the legato line.

In her recording of "Chanson triste," Maggie Teyte does a magnificent job assisted and supported by Gerald Moore. Her sense of style and her unique French articulation make one forgive the almost "oily" portamentos she uses in her efforts to keep the unbroken French vocal line. Even in a matter of a quarter-century, musical taste changes. What may have sounded right in 1941 may seem somewhat sentimental and overdone today, but Maggie Teyte's interpretation of "Chanson triste" is in the true spirit of the time of Duparc.

HECTOR BERLIOZ (1803–1869)

Hector Berlioz is best known for his operatic compositions, *La Damnation de Faust* and *Les Troyens,* and his Requiem, but his song cycle, *Nuits d'Été,* consisting of six poems by the romantic poet Théophile Gautier, has always been a wonderful challenge to the refined interpreter. Régine Crespin, the French soprano, made a fantastic recording of these songs with Ernest Ansermet. The collaboration of these two great artists is perfect, especially in "Le Spectre de la Rose" and "Absence," where Régine Crespin gives admirable expression to all the coloring and refined sensuousness of the poet and the composer. Though they are love poems to a girl and should really be sung by a man, there is no "male" recording that I can recommend.

CLAUDE DEBUSSY (1862–1918)

The songs of Claude Debussy are the epitome of French vocal music. There may be many French songs that are more inviting and more rewarding for the performer, but Debussy is unsurpassed in his delicacy, refinement, and conciseness of poetic phrase and in his understanding of the expressiveness of the voice as a musical medium. His contempt for the patterns of classical harmony and his early enthusiasm for the Wagnerian idiom place him side by side with Hugo Wolf. Debussy must be sung, like Wolf, with the utmost exactness, in both tempo and musical form.

Three poems by Paul Bourget, "Beau Soir" (Beautiful Evening), "Romance," and "Les Cloches" (The Bells), are fine examples of Debussy's use of intense legato to "caress" the lines of the poem. In "Beau Soir," the singer's mood must be one of overwhelming bliss about the beauty of this world, which he sooner or later will have to leave. In "Les Cloches," the bells make you think of your youth, and you must convey an illusion of sad memories, memories of days past when the withered leaves were still green. In "Romance," the lilies and their strong fragrance also evoke memories of a happy past. The calmness and nostalgia in the musical pattern of these three songs add to the mood of dreaminess and frailty that Debussy's music creates.

When you listen to the recording of Maggie Teyte and Alfred Cortot, two Debussy authorities who learned how to perform his music from the man himself, you will certainly hear a presentation that is sure and stark without being robust, and bright as day without being naïve (listen also to Gérard Souzay).

The liveliness and impishness of "Fantoches" (Puppets), poetry by Verlaine, gives us one side of the French *esprit* in the concise description of the marionette show. And the priceless "Ballade des Femmes de Paris" (Ballad of the Women of Paris), where the fifteenth-century poet François Villon gambols about in the sounds of the French words and brags about Parisian women who deserve a prize because they are such good talkers, is anything but a whining and sentimental story. It is a good example of the wit and fun that often occur in Debussy's songs (listen to Maggie Teyte or Gérard Souzay).

MAURICE RAVEL (1875–1937)

Don Quichotte à Dulcinée is a cycle of three songs based on poems by Paul Morand. Ravel, who was born in the Pyrenees, was very attracted, almost obsessed, by the exciting rhythmical elements found in Spanish music, as is evident in his admirable characterization of the Spanish dreamer and nobleman. Most male singers find it rewarding to personify Don Quichotte in his lovesick eulogies to fair Dulcinée; if done with elegance and lightness, it is a wonderful group to put on your concert program (listen to Gérard Souzay).

The exotic *Shéhérazade,* a setting of poems by Tristan Klingsor, also consists of three songs: "Asie" (Asia), "La Flûte Enchantée" (The enchanted flute), and "L'Indifférent" (The indifferent one), but it takes a most excellent musician and a technically skilled singer to perform them, for they are not easy. The clear and elaborate accompaniment evokes the atmosphere of the Orient. Régine Crespin gives an authentic presentation of these marvelous songs (listen also to Jennie Tourel).

FRANCIS POULENC (1899–1963)

Of the French vocal composers of more recent times, Francis Poulenc was fortunate to have worked closely with an authentic and excellent interpreter of his songs, the baritone Pierre Bernac. In 1965, I attended Pierre Bernac's master classes at the Mannes College of Music in New York on the subject of the French *mélodie.* He stressed again and again the importance of the sustained legato line that is so typical of the French song. The singer should be able to maintain this legato without falling into the terrible sentimental habit of "scooping." Bernac's refined articulation of the French words is the best example of "chanter aux lèvres" (to sing on the lips). In "Le Bestiaire" (The Bestiary), he manages to personify the dromedary, the carp, and the crab with great humor, while illustrating this point (listen to Pierre Bernac and Francis Poulenc and also to Bernhard Kruysen).

ENGLISH SONGS

JOHN DOWLAND (1563–1626)

England in the sixteenth, seventeenth, and eighteenth centuries produced great song composers. John Dowland and the other Elizabethan composers wrote their songs mostly to lute accompaniment. Dowland himself was one of the most accomplished lute virtuosi who ever lived. With their complicated rhythms and great technical demands, these songs present a challenge to the singer of today.

Also, their musical value and emotional impact have such a stimulating effect on both performer and listener that they are an exciting asset to every singer's repertoire. Even if they lose something in being accompanied by harpsichord (on the lute stop), some of these centuries-old songs sparkle like precious stones. "I Saw My Lady Weep," "Flow My Tears," "Fine Knacks for Ladies," "Shall I Sue," and "Come Again" are some of Dowland's best-known songs (listen to Julian Bream and Peter Pears).

HENRY PURCELL (1658–1695) and GEORGE FREDERICK HANDEL (1685–1759)

The present interest in and understanding of baroque music has resulted in a growing appreciation of the songs of Henry Purcell and George Frederick Handel. The originality and ingenuity of Purcell often strike one as being strangely modern. Because they give preference to the words and use all kinds of embellishments to elucidate the poetry, his songs are a joy to sing. Purcell was a gifted singer himself, even as a boy soprano. He was a chorister in the Chapel Royal in London and later sang the countertenor solo in one of his many odes to St. Cecilia, *Hail, Bright Cecilia,* written in 1692 (listen to Alfred Deller).

The operas and oratorios of Handel are filled with arias and songs in Italian, English, and German that can easily be sung out of context. Whether simple or complicated, they are all marvelously suited for the voice. With his international background, Handel acquired a thorough understanding of the possibilities of the human voice in Italy, in his native Germany, and in England. It is no wonder that his music is so translatable.

Sergius Kagen, in *Music for the Voice,** makes a fine classification of Handel's arias and songs. He says that the arias can be performed by voices other than those for which they were originally intended. As long as this does not involve male singers taking female roles, and vice versa, I agree with him.

RALPH VAUGHAN WILLIAMS (1872–1958)

It is a sad fact that most of the Victorian era was a dry and uninteresting period in England as far as the writing of music was concerned. Only with Ralph Vaughan Williams is there another great name in English vocal composing. His *Songs of Travel* (Robert L. Stevenson) are rewarding and not complicated. The song "The Vagabond" (number one of the cycle) calls for the same youthful exuberance as Schubert's "Das Wandern," with its combination of folk song patterns and original harmonies.

Vaughan Williams also set to music six poems by A. E. Housman in the cycle *On Wenlock Edge.* This work for tenor, piano, and

* New York: Holt, Rinehart & Winston, Inc., 1949, p. 115.

string quartet (*ad lib.*) is of rare originality and offers great possibilities for the singer who wants to be one of the "instruments" in a chamber music group.

In *Five Mystical Songs,* with words by the seventeenth-century poet George Herbert, Vaughan Williams succeeds in putting his own personal stamp on the music and yet evoking the style of the early Gregorian chants and hymns. The ideal performance of these religious songs is with chorus and full orchestra, but Vaughan Williams himself has indicated how they can be done without chorus and with piano accompaniment.

BENJAMIN BRITTEN (1913–)

Not since the days of Henry Purcell has there been such an original and prolific English composer as Benjamin Britten. Thanks to his close collaboration with Peter Pears, the outstanding tenor and musical interpreter, Britten has achieved a sovereignty in all his writing for the voice that is most exciting and personal.

Britten's standards are very high. He requires the singer to exercise all his vocal resources to their absolute limits. His operatic parts and the tenor solos in *Serenade for Tenor, Horn, and Strings,* in *Canticles I, II,* and *III,* and in the cycles *The Holy Sonnets of John Donne* and the *Seven Michelangelo Sonnets* require a simultaneous intensity and agility of voice that is unique in the world of music. The singer is often overwhelmed by Britten's deep understanding of and close adherence to the words, even when the poetry is in the archaic Italian of the Michelangelo sonnets (listen to Peter Pears).

On July 31, 1964, Benjamin Britten received the first Aspen Award. In his acceptance speech, he said the following, which I think is pertinent to the interpretation of music and the singer's art:

> Music does not exist in a vacuum. It does not exist until it is performed. . . . It is the quality which cannot be acquired simply by the exercise of a technique or a system. It is something to do with personality, with gift, with spirit. I simply call it magic! . . . Every time I come back to "Winterreise" I am amazed. The magic is renewed.
>
> The magic comes only with the sounding of the music, with the turning of the written notes into sound. . . . This magic can be said to consist of just the music that is *not* in the score. . . . A musical experience needs three human beings at least; it requires a composer, a performer, and a listener. . . . The loudspeaker . . . is not part of a true musical experience, it is simply a substitute. Music demands . . . as much effort on the listener's part as the two other corners of the triangle; *this holy triangle* of composer, performer, and listener.*

OTHER ART SONGS

To sing the songs of Modeste Musorgski (1839–1881) in Russian is an almost superhuman task for a non-Russian singer, and an ordeal, too, for a non-Russian audience. Some singers have undertaken this task, and it *does* add atmosphere and authenticity to the program, since the composer wrote the melody to fit the Russian language (as is the case with Schubert and German). The program notes have to be so long and complex, however, that the song will have come to the end before the audience has read them. When only a small minority of the audience is able to understand the Russian, I would compromise and sing Musorgski in English translation. I would not omit these dramatic songs from my repertoire. His cycles *In the Nursery* and *Songs and Dances of Death,*

* *Saturday Review,* 22 August 1964.

and the marvelous setting of Goethe's "Song of the Flea" take a very high place in song literature.

The songs of Yrjö Kilpinen, Jean Sibelius, Hugo Alfvén, Wilhelm Stenhammar, Edvard Grieg, Niels W. Gade, J. P. E. Hartmann, and Carl Nielsen are mostly written to Scandinavian texts, but can be sung in English translation. (Why should Grieg be sung in German in America? The Norwegians certainly would not like the idea. By the way, the famous "Jeg elsker dig" was written to a Danish poem by Hans Christian Andersen.) It seems to me that the majority of Carl Nielsen's songs in which he deliberately tries to be "folksy" are so closely bound to the Danish words that they lose too much if sung in English, though this is not true of his more complex songs. Some of the "romances" or ballads belonging to this group are of great musical interest and lasting value (listen to Flagstad, Nilsson, Borg, and Schiøtz).

The reason I have mentioned so few contemporary song composers is certainly not because I think the songs of Alban Berg, Anton Webern, Darius Milhaud, Paul Hindemith, Michael Head, Samuel Barber, or Ned Rorem are unimportant compositions. (I regard "I Hear an Army" by Samuel Barber and James Joyce as one of the greatest songs of this century.) But, it is the obligation of the performer and interpreter to make a quality selection, and to try these songs out "on the dog."

III

The Oratorio

THE TERM *oratorio* stems from the religious exercises performed in that room of a monastery called the *oratorium,* the hall of prayer. In Italian, the oratorio was called a *dramma sacro per musica* (a sacred drama for music). Its roots are in the liturgy of the Roman Catholic Church and special forms of it are actually part of the liturgy, for instance, the Requiem Mass for the dead.

The oldest form of oratorio is the so-called *Passion,* which concentrates on the suffering, death, and resurrection of Christ. In the Passions, the recitative of the Evangelist or narrator (Historicus) relates the Biblical text, which is interrupted at the dramatic highlights by arias or choruses commenting on the events from a human point of view.

The history of the oratorio is a long and great one, but the standard repertoire today is relatively small.

GEORGE FREDERICK HANDEL (*1685–1759*)

Handel's English oratorios, which form the nucleus of the oratorio as a genre, enjoy enormous popularity today. Their subjects are mostly taken from the Bible: *Samson, Saul, Judas Maccabeus,* and the *Messiah.* The solo parts contain rich psychological characterizations of these Biblical personalities.

The great choruses that abound in all Handel's oratorios show the composer's deep understanding of the possibilities of the human voice. Their majestic power and fine proportions make them a model for all choral composition.

In *Saul,* one of the most magnificent of the many oratorios Handel wrote, we encounter some of the finest character painting in all musical literature—opera and art song included. *Saul* is so highly dramatic that it should perhaps be relabeled "opera" and staged theatrically.

In his outstanding work on Handel, Paul Henry Lang writes: "*Saul* . . . is pure tragedy without a trace of religious philosophy."* Saul himself possesses all the frailties of the human character: vanity, lust for power, jealousy, and even hatred. He throws his javelin against both Jonathan, his own son, and David, who tries to alleviate his depression with song and harp-playing. His monologue, "Wretch as I am! Of my own ruin author!" depicts the man who is well aware of his own falsehood and baseness. The singer who performs the bass phrases of Saul must try to embody all of these complexities. The closer he adheres to Handel's music, the more likely he is to succeed.

The *Messiah* belongs to the personal heritage of every English-speaking person from his earliest school days and has become part of the cultural background not only of musicians but of educated persons in all nations. This great work retains its freshness and originality in spite of being performed every year in every country *and* with every possible interpretation. In 1951, Felix Raugel, the French oratorio authority, gave a performance of this English Protestant work in a Catholic Church in Casablanca, Morocco, in French with French singers and a Danish tenor!

The singers of Handel's time used embellishments and appoggiaturas lavishly. I doubt, however, that we should attempt historical correctness in this respect. Besides, today's fastidious musicians, be it right or wrong, would probably not be able to accept everything that was done by the Handelian singers. We should, however, get as close as possible to the heart and core of Handel's music in our performances.

* *George Frederic Handel* (New York: W. W. Norton & Company, Inc., 1966), p. 303.

Misinterpretations of Handel's perfect phrases can often be heard in performances of the *Messiah* today. Strange ritardandi and fermate are strewn all through the score because the singers say, "this is the way we *feel* it in our church," and Handel's greatness is thereby foolishly obscured.

The tenor's recitative "Comfort ye, my people" and the aria "Every valley shall be exalted" open the work after the short, stately overture.

The first "Comfort ye" should be sung preferably *on* the beat,

simultaneously with the chord, freely phrased but without distortion of the rhythmical pattern. The orchestra echoes this rubato phrase but sets the beginning tempo immediately at the following measure. The third "Comfort ye" is *ad lib.*, as prescribed, then back to tempo. The third line "and cry unto her" is also rubato, but with the two eighth notes "that her" leading into tempo again.

and cry un-to_her that her war - fare, her war - fare is ac-com-plished,
p

In what I would call the "real" recitative, "The voice of him that crieth in the wilderness, Prepare ye the way of the Lord, Make straight in the desert a highway for our God," the prophet's cry constitutes the central idea of the whole work. Here the singer might use a broad and dignified phrasing, but he must definitely observe every one of the long rests. The rests add to the grandeur of the prophet's line, which would be completely ruined by hurrying. The architecture of the phrase is strengthened by placing the chords *on* the beats, but this is not always done. The final two chords must be on the second and third beats to avoid a dissonance that Handel certainly did not intend.

The tempo of the aria "Every valley" is twice as fast as that of the recitative (suggested MM: ♪=96 and ♩=96). This enables the singer to handle the runs in one phrase, as Handel obviously intended. It also gives the aria the necessary elastic lightness. Not until the middle of this long oratorio does the tenor return with

The voice of him that cri - eth in the
wil - der-ness, Pre - pare ye the way of the Lord, make
straight in the de-sert a high-way for our God.

two recitatives and two arias forming a beautiful unity. They should be sung lyrically and *sotto voce* as indicated (suggested MM for "Behold, and see," ♪=84; for "But thou didst not leave his soul," ♩=63).

For the final tenor aria, "Thou shalt break them," a trumpetlike voice with sound and fury is called for (suggested MM: ♩=104).

For the five powerful bass arias, with their accompanying recitatives, a very flexible, cellolike bass voice is needed. The bass coloraturas must be sung with elegance and lightness; otherwise they will sound like an elephant dance. (Suggested MM's for these arias are as follows: "But who may abide," ♪=92, and the middle section, 𝅗𝅥=92; "The people that walked in darkness," ♪=120; "Thou art gone up on high," ♩=126; "Why do the nations," ♩=132; "The trumpet shall sound," ♩=116.)

The arias for alto were written for a contralto singer, Mrs. Cibber, not for a castrato. In his fine recording of the *Messiah,* however, Leonard Bernstein uses Russell Oberlin, the countertenor, for the part and accomplishes an instrumental and vibratoless musical line, but the sound of the female voice is to be preferred. (Listen to and compare two different recordings of this passage: Kathleen Ferrier singing one and Russell Oberlin singing the other.)

In the short recitative "Behold! A virgin shall conceive," Kathleen Ferrier's voice still rings vividly in my ear from our *Messiah* performances in Liverpool in 1945. She sang it with all the effective rests, thus obtaining the strong feeling of "God with us."

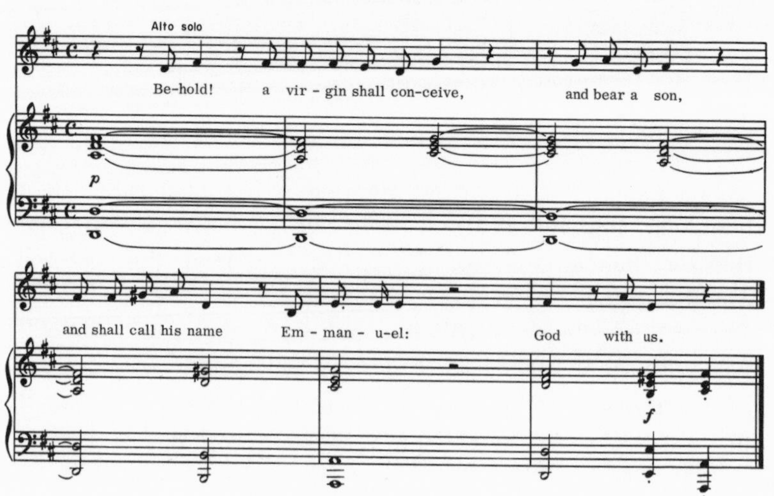

The pastoral character and moving tempo of the aria "He shall feed his flock" and "Come unto Him," which is divided between the contralto and the soprano, constitute one of the highlights in which the clear soprano sound enters after the darker, lower voice (suggested MM: ♩.=50, *not* the frequently heard boring tempo in slow twelfths, in which the character of pastorale is completely lost).

The contralto reaches the climax of the whole work's beauty and wonder with the aria "He was despised and rejected." It is no less than a musical crime to omit, as is often done, the fast "He gave his back to the smiters." Apart from the exciting quality of this short part, the chords that begin the repeat are magnificent.

When the tenor and contralto join in the subdued and still victorious duet "O, Death where is thy sting?" the singers should give expression to the deep religious feeling of this part.

The soprano, poor she!, has to wait for an hour or so before she enters with the seraphic recitative, "There were shepherds abiding in the field." Tenor, bass, and contralto arias and the most wonderful choruses have filled up the work until now.

The great coloratura aria "Rejoice, rejoice greatly" (suggested MM: ♩=104), with its long runs, like pearls on a string, is a real test of the soprano voice that is right for the *Messiah*.

The singer must feel four beats (and not twelve!) in the next soprano aria, "How beautiful are the feet," or it becomes pedestrian.

The aria "I know that my Redeemer liveth" (suggested MM: ♩=96) loses all its *jubiloso* character if it is sung too slowly, as it usually is.

Do not rush the tempo of "And though worms destroy his body." Hurrying will (and frequently does) totally ruin all the monumental greatness of these macabre words.

The last soprano aria, "If God be for us," is seldom heard, and this is too bad. It sums up the Christian idea with the characteristic Handelian simplicity of the melodic line (listen to the *Messiah* conducted by Colin Davis).

JOHANN SEBASTIAN BACH (1685–1750)

The soloist in any Bach cantata, oratorio, or passion should always keep in mind what Bach wrote in all his compositions, "Soli Deo Gloria" (Praise be to God alone). With their deeply religious and introspective character, Bach's works present a strong contrast to Handel's English oratorios. Actually, Bach's are closer to the original conception of an oratorio.

Bach's two monumental works, the *Johannespassion* (The Passion According to St. John), composed in 1723, and the *Matthäuspassion* (The Passion According to St. Matthew), composed in 1729, overshadow all his other vocal compositions. It is hard to imagine how Bach managed to perform these with the small forces he had at his disposal in St. Thomas Church in Leipzig. Today their original structure and proportions are often obscured in performances with huge orchestras and choruses.

In both works, the phrases of the various dramatis personae all require detailed characterizations: Pilate, the Roman governor, cold and yet worried about the rebel, Jesus; the High Priest, anxious to prove Jesus guilty of blasphemy and high treason; and Peter, the weak disciple who denies Jesus three times. The fiendishly difficult and elaborate arias and the great choruses are musical inserts that comment on the tragic events from a human-pietistic point of view.

The baritone who is chosen to sing the part of Christ must approach his phrases with awe and humility. He must try to endow his singing with a loftiness and dignity in order to do justice to the divine character of the words. The part represents both God's Son and the man suffering on the cross, and it must be sung with serene simplicity and restrained passion (listen to Gérard Souzay, Heinz Rehfuss, or Friedrich Schorr). These three singers all have the true attitude of awe, humility, and understanding of the representation of divinity. Friedrich Schorr possesses that rare quality in his voice that is the gift of few singers, that goes directly to the heart and almost makes you weep. I would call it soul or divine spirit.

The most characteristic feature of the passion is the Evangelist's part. His narration of the Gospel runs through the whole of both oratorios and binds the many sections together.

The language of the passions is the old German of the Protestant Bible, and Bach formed his recitatives after the rhythm of this language. The narrator must follow Bach's declamation in telling the story, dramatic as it is, in an objective way. The right kind of voice for this part is that of a minister or priest when he uses "plain song" (parlando!) in reading the Gospel. The singer must use an impersonal, instrumental, and flexible tone, often characterized by the word "white," because he intentionally avoids all coloring and holds back any personal emotions. Karl Erb, Max Meili, Helmut Krebs, Fritz Wunderlich, Blake Stern, and others have given model evidence of the controlled way this precarious and taxing part of the Evangelist should be sung. Karl Erb was the ideal narrator. He sang, not from the score, but from the Bible itself, and preached the Gospel through Bach's unmatched recitative.

The tessitura is extremely high, especially in the *St. Matthew Passion*. The reason for this is that the pitch has been raised one to one and a half tones (approximate frequency A: 415 to 440), since Bach's time, which may be fine for instruments, but it is cruel on the human voice.

The Evangelist's recitative introduces one person after another and describes the dramatic events.

Before concerning yourself with the vocal or musical problems of the works, read the texts aloud, not from the score, but from your own written copy. The following is from the *St. John Passion*, nos. 16–18.

EVANGELIST: *Und Hannas sandte ihn gebunden zu dem Hohenpriester Caiphas; Simon Petrus stund und wärmete sich, da sprachen sie zu ihm:*

CHORUS: *Bist du nicht seiner Jünger einer?*
EVANGELIST: *Er leugnete aber und sprach:*
PETRUS: *Ich bin's nicht!*
EVANGELIST: *Spricht des Hohenpriesters Knecht einer, ein Gefreund'ter des, dem Petrus das Ohr abgehauen hatte:*
DIENER: *Sahe ich dich nicht im Garten bei ihm?*
EVANGELIST: *Da verleugnete Petrus abermal, und alsobald krähete der Hahn. Da gedachte Petrus an die Worte Jesu, und ging hinaus und weinete bitterlich.*

EVANGELIST: Now Annas ordered Jesus bound, and then sent him bound to Caiphas. Simon Peter stood, still warming himself. Then said they unto him:
CHORUS: Art thou not one of his disciples?
PETER: I am not!
EVANGELIST: Then saith one of the high priest's followers, being kinsman of him whom Peter had smitten and cut his ear off:
SERVANT: Did I not see thee in the garden with him?
EVANGELIST: Then did Peter deny it a third time, and straightaway the cock began his crowing. Then did Peter bring to mind the word of Jesus, and he went out bewailing it bitterly.

When you now look at Bach's music, you will realize how closely he follows the prosody of the language and how his numerous modulations imitate the varied colorings of the dramatic spoken word. However, on rare occasions Bach makes the narrator get carried away, so that he, without any transition, moves into a measured adagio arioso.

Listen to the *St. Matthew Passion* conducted by Mogens Wöldike, and the *St. John Passion* conducted by Karl Forster. The musicianship and artistry of Mogens Wöldike is exquisite. The strict and lucid quality of the music in the *St. Matthew Passion* is genuine

Bach, and the person who is performing it always steps back and pays homage to this great music.

The performing singer can learn a good deal from this essential attitude.

In Karl Forster's recording of the *St. John Passion,* I especially recommend that you listen to Fritz Wunderlich's reciting of the Evangelist's part and to Fischer-Dieskau's true understanding of the phrases of Christ.

FRANZ JOSEPH HAYDN (1732–1809)

While in Bach the "Soli Deo Gloria" stands as a motto for all his works, and the singer has an obligation to give a straightforward and humble expression to Bach's pietistic—and pious—music, Haydn's oratorios open up a completely new side of music. Freshness, humor, and joy of life are the undertone and the texture.

In his oratorio *Die Schöpfung* (The Creation), Haydn composed his music to the German translation of an adaptation of John Milton's *Paradise Lost.* The work can be beautifully performed in both languages, and the problems of the musical form are much fewer than in Handel and Bach. Simple harmonies and easily accessible melodies account for the enormous popularity of this work. The many descriptions of nature in *Die Schöpfung* are something new in an oratorio.

The three archangels, Gabriel (soprano), Uriel (tenor), and Raphael (bass), give happy descriptions of the Creator's work, and the splendid choruses join in the great marvels. The dark, dignified phrases of the bass voice announce the Creation itself, but then with the first beam of light the tenor sings the aria "Nun schwanden vor dem heiligen Strahle" (Now vanish, before the holy beams).

The short recitative before this aria should be sung with a bright and light voice, not slowly with long final notes. Get off them. It sets the stage for the joyous sound of Uriel's phrases whenever they reappear. The light pickup notes and the bouncing rhythm are indicated by the orchestral accompaniment. Sing with the freshness of a surprised child.

Raphael, the bass, now begins the description of the acts of creation. First, the dividing of land and water. Sing like a cello, both legato and pizzicato. "Die Fläche, weit gedehnt, durchläuft der breite Strom in mancher Krümme" (Thro' th'open plains out-

f
Hier schiesst der ge-len- ki-ge Ti - ger em-por.
3
Mit flie- gen- der Mäh- ne springt und
wieh'rt voll Mut und Kraft das ed - le Ross.

stretching wide, in serpent error rivers flow). The calmly flowing river could only be legato. But earlier, when Raphael sings about "der leichte flockige Schnee" (the light and flaky snow), he should sing simply staccato.

All through the vivid bass recitative about the creation of the various animals—lion, tiger, stag, horse, cattle, sheep, insects, and the snakes—the orchestra helps and instructs the musically sensitive singer by giving the "cue" in imitation of the animals' characteristics.

The fulfillment of the Creation, the *creation of man,* is described in the magnificent tenor aria as "Mit Würd und Hoheit." The ascending nonlegato line, "steht der Mensch ein Mann und König der Natur" (In native worth stands a Man, the lord and king of nature all) should be sung in a victorious and proud manner—like a trumpet.

URIEL
Mit
Ob.
p
Würd und Ho-heit an - ge-tan, mit Schön-heit, Stärk und_ Mut be-gabt, gen
Him-mel_ auf-ge - rich - tet, steht der Mensch, ein
cresc.
Mann und Kö - nig_ der Na - tur.
f
f
Fag.

"Put a mute in the trumpet," when you sing about the creation of woman. Make it *piano* and legato. Gabriel, a lyrical, light, and warm soprano voice sings about the green meadows, fragrant flowers, plants, and fruit trees in her first *angelic* aria, "Nun beut die Flur" (With verdure clad). Take the exact tempo of the introduction, andante, and let your voice, with a light pickup note, continue the melody of the oboe and bassoon, as if you added still another instrument. Bring all your musicianship into use and sing as if you were a flute.

As was the case in Handel's oratorios, any distortion of the rhythmical pattern or melodic line should be avoided. Don't try to express your own ideas dictated by vocal ambition, but try to do justice to Haydn's music. A perfect vocal technique is absolutely necessary for "Nun beut die Flur" and for the other great soprano aria, "Auf starkem Fittiche" (On mighty wings). In both arias, the very long-held notes ask for secure breath control, and the extensive runs ask for lightness. You must also be able to make a perfect trill where Haydn simply imitates the cooing of "the tender dove."

Twice the three soloists join in ensembles in which a true chamber music effect should be obtained. As in an instrumental trio, the three singers must listen to each other in order to realize who has the theme, i.e., when each has to bring out his voice and when he has to hold back. Sometimes it is not too easy to decide who has the most important line, as all three voices have melodious phrases (listen to *Die Schöpfung* conducted by Mogens Wöldike).

Haydn's other oratorio, *Die Jahreszeiten* (1807–1810), which is based on James Thomson's poem *The Seasons,* could actually be called a *Singspiel* (comic opera) without any sacred character. You might as well regard it as four secular cantatas, even if it is composed within the frame of an oratorio with solos, ensembles, and choruses.

The baritone who sings Simon's aria "Schon eilet froh der

GABRIEL
Den O - dem hauchst du wie-der aus,
URIEL
Den O - dem hauchst du wie-der aus,
RAPHAEL
Den O - dem hauchst du wie-der aus,
p
und neu - es Le - ben_ sprosst her - vor.
und neu - es Le - ben sprosst_ her - vor.
und neu - es Le - ben sprosst her - vor.
Fl. Klar.
p
Klar.
Fag.

Ackersmann" (With eagerness the husbandman) should express the same joy of life and simple happiness you find in the opening song of Franz Schubert's *Die schöne Müllerin*—"Das Wandern ist des Müllers Lust" (To Wander Is The Miller's Joy)—which was written about fifteen years later. To express the idyllic *Gemütlichkeit* (joviality) and good nature of this early romantic pure music is a good schooling for the singer who wants to prepare himself for the performance of works of a later date.

Schon ei - let froh der Ac - kers-mann zur_ Ar - beit auf das Feld,
p
p
p
p

Das Wan - dern ist des Mül - lers_ Lust, das Wan - dern!
p
mf

It is easier to sing "O, Fleiss, von dir kommt alles Heil" (O, Industry, from Thee springs every good), with its rationalistic and dry philosophy, when it is set to this happy and beautiful music.

The tenor, Lukas, a young peasant, and the soprano, Hanne, join in a pretty and respectable love duet: "Welch ein Glück ist treue Liebe" (What a delight is true love) (listen to *Die Jahreszeiten* conducted by Karl Böhm).

Without possessing the depth and majesty of most of Handel's oratorios, these two works of Haydn form the link between Handel and Mendelssohn.

FELIX MENDELSSOHN (1809–1847)

Mendelssohn, who rescued Bach's Passions from oblivion, wrote the great oratorio *Elijah,* with Biblical text. The sweet, flowing melodiousness and full harmonies of the genuine romantic period characterize the recitatives, arias, and big choruses of this work.

In Handel's baroque and Haydn's rococo music, the singer must strive for objectivity and closely follow the note picture, but in Mendelssohn he has a larger scope for expressing his own personal feelings in his interpretation, a characteristic of romantic music. This proves to be a danger to the singer who often feels tempted to overemphasize and sentimentalize this romantic but tasteful music.

In *Elijah,* the prophet is a powerful baritone. This part must be sung with conviction and dignity so that the audience is awed by his fearless spiritual strength.

In Handel's *Messiah,* I suggested a trumpetlike tenor for the aria "Thou shalt break them." This aria bears a distinct resemblance to Elijah's aria "Is not His word like a fire?" where a trombonelike baritone is more appropriate.

In the great aria "Hear Ye, Israel! Hear what the Lord speaketh," Mendelssohn lets the soprano sing the words of God, which is unusual. It takes a highly dramatic soprano voice to do this with authority and emphasis.

The recitatives and arias of Obadiah, the tenor, can be sung with great effect and beauty. Obadiah speaks for God and admonishes Israel. He quotes God's promises to His people in the aria, "If with all your hearts ye truly seek me." Of the few arias for alto, the simple, almost choralelike "O, rest in the Lord" gives the singer ample opportunity for legato phrasing and warm, peaceful expression.

Using the English Bible translation, *Elijah* had a great success in England right from its first performance, which was commissioned for the Birmingham Festival (1846). It still enjoys popularity (listen to *Elijah* in English conducted by Joseph Krips).

The Requiems of MOZART, BRAHMS, *and* VERDI

It is very interesting and rewarding to compare the requiems of the three great composers, Mozart, Brahms, and Verdi. All three works were written during a period when the composers were obsessed by the themes of death and finality.

Wolfgang Amadeus Mozart (1756–1791) died before finishing his Requiem; one of his highly talented pupils finished it for him. Starting with the opening bars of no. 7, "Lacrymosa," this pupil, Xaver Süssmayr, used Mozart's own sketches to make a successful unity of this marvelous work.

Ein deutsches Requiem (A German Requiem) was begun by Johannes Brahms (1833–1897) in 1868, a period when he was deeply saddened by the insanity and death of his close friend Robert Schumann. Brahms added Part V later, in memory of his mother. Formally, *Ein deutsches Requiem* has very little to do with the traditional sections of the Mass; the Old Testament texts are all concentrated on the topic of Life and Death. A soprano and a baritone are the only soloists in this mainly choral work.

The Requiem of Giuseppe Verdi (1813–1901) is a nonliturgical work created within the framework of the Mass for the dead, with all the imagination and dramatic sense of this great opera writer.

The work, composed in memory of the Italian poet Alessandro Manzoni, had its first performance in 1874, with Verdi conducting.

The serene classicism of Mozart's mass makes a strong contrast to the other two. Brahms's work, with its full harmonies, both in the orchestral accompaniment and in the choruses, and Verdi's effective and almost operatic colorfulness require rich and strong voices and true vocal mastery, where the strict rococo music of Mozart must be sung with instrumental lightness and flexibility. The soprano part should have an almost superhuman, seraphic character. (Listen to Mozart's Requiem conducted by Bruno Walter, Verdi's Requiem conducted by Fritz Reiner, and Brahms's *Ein deutsches Requiem* conducted by Otto Klemperer. All three works, widely different in style as they are, are excitingly performed by conductors Walter, Klemperer, and Reiner, and singers Seefried, Tourel, Simoneau, Schwarzkopf, Fischer-Dieskau, Price, Elias, Tozzi, and the incomparable Björling.)

A great number of recent composers have been involved in creating a renaissance of the oratorio. The singer of today should be familiar with Arthur Honegger's *Le Roi David* (King David) (1921) and *Jeanne d'Arc au Bûcher* (Joan of Arc at the Stake) (1935), Igor Stravinsky's *Oedipus Rex* (King Oedipus) (1927) and *The Flood* (1962), William Walton's *Belshazzar's Feast* (1931), Michael Tippett's *A Child of Our Time* (1941), Frank Martin's *In Terra Pax* (1944), Sergei Prokofiev's *On Guard for Peace* (1950), and Carl Orff's *Comoedia de Christi Resurrectione* (1955).

BENJAMIN BRITTEN (1913–)

Benjamin Britten's *War Requiem* (1962) is a most important contemporary work. The English poems of Wilfred Owen are inserted between the Latin sections of the Requiem Mass to form a unique and unusual whole. The *War Requiem* was written for the consecration of the rebuilt Coventry Cathedral, which was destroyed during World War II by German bombs. For the recording, Britten had a Russian soprano, a German baritone, and a British tenor singing the solo parts. In the *War Requiem,* the Latin texts of the masses must be sung with pious, but impersonal devotion; the Owen poems, however, are passionately subjective and require deep poetic understanding from the soloists. In the various Requiem Mass sections, the soprano represents the Christian concept, and her part is extremely demanding. The tenor and the baritone share the Owen poems and symbolize humanity. In his poem, Owen changed the Biblical story and let Abraham kill his son, "And half the seed of Europe, one by one!" Britten used this idea ingeniously in his *War Requiem* (listen to the performance conducted by Britten with Galina Vishnevskaya, Dietrich Fischer-Dieskau, and Peter Pears).

KRZYSZTOF PENDERECKI (1933–)

The Polish composer Krzysztof Penderecki wrote his *Passion According to Saint Luke* in 1966 for the seven hundredth anniversary of the cathedral in Münster, Germany.

Penderecki uses an actor to narrate the Evangelist's part, and the Latin words are spoken in such a way as to point up their close relation to the archaic liturgical chant. The solo parts (soprano, baritone, and bass) are molded in the traditional form, yet they are a deeply moving example of contemporary composition for solo voices at its best.

The soprano's wild, plaintive tones express the fathomless tragedy of humanity. Christ is sung by a baritone, as he is in Bach's Passions. His prayer in Gethsemane, "Pater, si vis, transfer calicem istum a me" (Father, if you will, take this chalice away from me), carries a message from all the innocent victims of violence and tyranny. Here Penderecki creates an unusual contrast by using the rich speaking voice of the Evangelist against the singing passages of the baritone. *Turba,* the mob, traditionally done by the chorus, is a truly noisy crowd, where *Sprechstimme* (speaking voice), accompanied by instruments, is used extensively.

The cold authoritative bass of Pilate interrupts the crowd: "Tu es rex Judaeorum?" (Are you the King of the Jews?). This question stands out like lightning and thunder, and Penderecki achieves an almost frightening effect with his strong and striking accent on *orum.*

This Passion is perhaps the strongest expression of the sufferings of an entire nation that has ever been written. In it, Penderecki has given voice to the martyrdom of Poland during World War II, with music that has an overpowering and shattering effect. I predict that this Passion will become one of the most important contributions to the sacred music literature of our time (listen to the *Passion According to Saint Luke* conducted by Czyz).

IV

Opera

OPERA is a drama in which one sings instead of speaks. The Italian expression for an opera, *dramma per musica* (drama for music), illustrates this very clearly. Even though operatic music forms the bulk of vocal literature, it falls, theoretically speaking, outside the frame of this book about the singer's art. There are several reasons for this.

Opera is theater, and in the performance of an opera, in the very staging of the "show," the singer himself is only part of a whole, and consequently only responsible for his own part of the finished product.

The conductor has the final word about the performance of the opera, and all the singers must be obedient to his ideas about musical form, style, and tempi, and perhaps about the singing itself.

The operatic singer should first and foremost be an actor and perform his part according to the rules of acting, and he should be trained accordingly.

However, when singing the solo parts—arias and recitatives—in an operatic role, interpretation plays a major role in making the part a personal artistic contribution. Thus the operatic singer should be equally familiar with the techniques of acting and the techniques of interpretative singing.

Every voice student has to learn many arias from various operas. Usually he owns collections of operatic arias and practices these as part of his education. Does he know the background of these arias? Does his teacher require that he be familiar with the whole opera, with the particular part to which the arias belong? Is he fully aware of the special dramatic climax in the opera for which the particular aria is an expression?

The study and practice of any aria must begin with the study of the entire opera. Only when the student has a very clear picture of the background of the arias should he sing them.

Unfortunately, operatic arias are included in the current recital repertoire. It is understandable, because most arias document the singer's vocal skills and techniques, his musicianship, and other potentials, but in my opinion it is basically wrong to perform arias outside the context of the whole opera. The piano accompaniments arranged from the orchestral score of an opera are more often than not a very mediocre substitute.

The first attempts to express the thoughts and emotions of the characters in a drama with singing and music were made by people like Jacopo Peri and Claudio Monteverdi in the early seventeenth century.

The true bel canto singing needed in these operas indicates that preference was given to the vocal sound, which had to express everything in early Italian operas.

In his *Music in Western Civilization,* Paul Henry Lang rightly says that those first operas (e.g., Claudio Monteverdi's *L'Incoronazione di Poppea*) possessed the true quality of a musical drama. He speaks about ". . . the intensity of dramatization through the singing voice," and calls *Poppea* ". . . opera in its unique and most glorious domain."* (Listen to *L'Incoronazione di Poppea* by Ewerhart.)

From Henry Purcell's *Dido and Aeneas* (1689) to the operas of today such as Alban Berg's *Wozzeck* (1921) and Benjamin Britten's *Peter Grimes* (1945), there is a wealth of styles and attitudes toward musical expression with which the operatic singer must become familiar (listen to *Dido and Aeneas* conducted by Anthony Lewis).

* New York: W. W. Norton & Company Inc., 1941, p. 351.

As in art song and oratorio, you should be fully acquainted with the social background of the respective periods, whether the opera is in the time of the gay Italian *commedia dell'arte,* as is the case with Giovanni Battista Pergolesi's opera *La serva padrona* from 1733, or the confused European scene after World War II, as in Gian Carlo Menotti's *The Consul* from 1950 (listen to *La serva padrona* by Pomeriggi Ettore Ciracis). Usually plots for opera are highly emotional and dramatic. The whole setup—orchestra, arias, choruses, ensembles, and recitatives—requires actions of an unusual or exalted character. Gods and half-gods, ancient kings, queens, and princes, medieval and renaissance episodes, and utopian settings are found in abundance in opera.

To bring an operatic role to the stage requires more than just a fine singing voice. Perhaps our generation demands more from an operatic singer than ever before. Earlier, enormously fat singers obtained success and world fame through their singing alone, and bad acting, or no acting at all, was forgiven. Today every young singer with ambitions for an opera career has to realize that it takes more than just voice to succeed. John Forsell, who was general manager of the Stockholm Opera in Sweden from 1913 to 1938, wanted his singers to be physically fit and good-looking. He insisted dictatorially that they go on a diet if they were too fat. "I will not tolerate men on the stage who look like pregnant females," he used to say.

Today an opera workshop is part of the curriculum of practically all music schools and conservatories. In these workshops, you, the student, will have ample opportunity to decide if you have the many-faceted potential for this most complex of careers. In the opera workshop you will be trained in stage deportment. The simple act of walking naturally and freely on a stage is a stumbling stone to many. You will have to learn dancing, gymnastics, and often fencing in order to develop and control the movements of your body. You will be taught how to use gestures to convey anger, sorrow, love, and joy.

You will be trained in using facial expressions, so that they never appear to be "put on," but are strong expressions of your own emotions and thoughts. You will learn to sing in many strange positions: lying down, kneeling, embracing, etc., and not merely standing securely at the piano, as in the singing studio.

In addition you will learn how to use make-up as an important device in characterization. Costumes are essential, too, to character delineation, and you will have to learn how to wear a costume gracefully and naturally. A medieval knight in full armor cannot walk like a young man in blue jeans, nor does the Queen of the Night behave like a girl in a miniskirt.

Theoretically, operatic voices are pigeonholed into all sorts of subdivisions. Among the so-called dramatic voices are the *Heldentenor* (the heroic tenor), the dramatic soprano, the heavy baritone, the contralto, and the basso profundo. Lyrical voices include coloratura sopranos and light tenors.

In most cases the size of the voice is the factor that determines whether the young singer goes into opera. A smallish voice, however beautiful and musical, cannot be heard in a large opera house in competition with a full orchestra. Another deciding factor is the singer's ability to *project* his voice and let it be "carried" by the orchestra. However, his acting ability and stage appearance are equally important.

An attraction to the theatrical world and a primitive desire to disguise oneself as another person often make young singers undertake to learn operatic repertoire without having the prerequisites for dramatic singing. Much money and years of struggle may be wasted in a vain effort to succeed in one of the most difficult of careers. Teachers, therefore, have an obligation to encourage only those young singers in whom dramatic talent and vocal and personal gifts abound.

Interpreting an operatic role is different from interpreting either an art song or an oratorio. In an opera the goal must be to personify, or "act," the role in vocal characterization as well as in appearance. In an art song and an oratorio the singer expresses, without acting, the thoughts and feeling that lie in the words alone.

Regrettably, poor acting is frequently seen on the operatic stage, but often the voice itself contains such musical intensity and dramatic energy that the audience is willing to overlook this flaw. Jussi Björling was not a good actor, and yet he was one of the greatest operatic singers of our time because of the great dramatic quality of his voice.

In the art song the singer is simply a mouthpiece for the poet and the composer. Many singers are not sufficiently aware of this basic difference between opera and art songs, although such great singers as Julius Patzak, Irmgard Seefried, Gerhardt Hüsch, Friedrich Schorr, Victoria de los Angeles, Heinrich Schlusnus, Elisabeth Schumann, Elisabeth Schwarzkopf, Dietrich Fischer-Dieskau, and others have shown that they could switch from one interpretational technique to the other.

After I had had the great experience of singing under the inspiring leadership of Fritz Busch, the well-known conductor, I was invited to audition for Mozart operas in Glyndebourne, England. I discussed with Busch the possibility of combining my career as a Lieder singer with that of an operatic tenor. Can one do both?

"No," was his blunt answer.

"Not even Mozart?"

"Yes, perhaps," he said.

The great dramatic artist, Lotte Lehmann, is a striking example of Fritz Busch's theory. She does not "switch" techniques, but carries her operatic conception of interpretation into her Lieder singing. "She turns the concert podium into an opera stage!" someone once said enthusiastically, which is exactly what I think should not be done.

An opera performance is a complex of many factors. As a young singer, therefore, you should go slowly at first. Start by learning the small roles and putting them in the proper relationships to the other parts. They are important for the unfolding of the drama as a whole.

The coach will not only teach you the music; he will also give you the over-all picture of the opera. What may at first appear as one big confusing jigsaw puzzle soon becomes less complicated under his guidance.

The stage director arranges the play on the stage, "blocks" it, as it is called. He tells you when to enter, where to walk, where to turn, which gestures to use. He gives you many instructions concerning the minutest details. He will call a great many rehearsals after the coach has taught all the singers their parts. Only during the last rehearsals and the dress rehearsal will you wear costume and make-up; only then will proper light be thrown at you as you perform against the background of the right sets and with the right props. Until then, you will have to use a great deal of imagination.

On stage the singer must learn to project his voice to the audience in the hall in such a manner that it still looks as if he is addressing his fellow actors. When the rehearsal piano is finally replaced by the orchestra, the conductor's first aim is to make the musicians familiar with *his* conception of the score and with the vocal sounds coming from the stage. The singers will have an awful feeling of being neglected until the conductor is ready to combine all the factors of the complete performance.

If the singer understands how to make the most of all the guidance and advice he has received, he can add his own talent to the role assigned him and make it a personal and valuable creation.

As to the thorough study of opera, there is a wealth of literature. Donald J. Grout's *A Short History of the Opera** is highly recommended as a basic study for all singers and students of opera.

Ernest Newman's *Stories of the Great Operas*† gives not only the contents of the librettos but also valuable information on the social and musical background of the separate operas.

The five principal periods, or "highlights," in the history of opera

* New York: Columbia University Press, 1965.

† New York: Alfred A. Knopf, Inc., 1930.

are the works of Mozart; the works of Rossini, Donizetti, Bellini, and Cherubini; Beethoven's *Fidelio* and Weber's *Der Freischütz*; the so-called grand operas by Gounod, Bizet, Massenet, and Puccini; and the operas by Verdi, Wagner, Debussy, and Richard Strauss.

WOLFGANG AMADEUS MOZART (1756–1791)

It is a common mistake of the voice student to think that he will be on the safe side if he chooses to perform Mozart because of its apparent simplicity. Nothing is more difficult and demanding to bring out than the sublime and serene style of Mozart's music. The singer must pay full respect to the musical structure, yet the vitality of the Mozart idiom must never suffer. The young singer, preferably led by the hand of some experienced musical artist, must approach Mozart's ingenious creations with great humility. All singers, from the highest coloratura sopranos to the lowest bassos, must be able to sing with perfect flexibility and lightness, and with the strictest precision as well. Furthermore, they *must* be able to act. It is almost painful to attend the elegant rococo Mozart operas when the singers are poor actors. In his *History of Music in Performance,* Frederick Dorian writes, "If Mozart's singers, no matter how celebrated, were lacking in acting ability, he held them in contempt and was ready to admonish them with very profane language."*

The light soubrette (maid servant) sopranos—Papagena in *Die Zauberflöte* (The Magic Flute), Zerlina in *Don Giovanni,* Despina in *Così fan tutte,* and Susanna in *Le Nozze di Figaro* (The Marriage of Figaro)—must be vivacious, dainty, and pretty. The lyric, almost dramatic, sopranos—Contessa in *Figaro* and Donna Anna and Donna Elvira in *Don Giovanni*—should, ideally, be tall, mature, good-looking women, with voices of great intensity and sonor-

* New York: W. W. Norton & Company, Inc., 1942, p. 275.

ity. Tamino in *Zauberflöte*, Ferrando in *Così fan tutte*, Don Ottavio in *Don Giovanni*, and Belmonte in *Die Entführung aus dem Serail* are fascinating, lyrical tenor parts, which ask for great acting abilities. The baritones Papageno in *Zauberflöte*, Figaro in *Figaro*, and Leporello in *Don Giovanni* are prototypes of the actor-singer and should not be considered by the singer who doesn't feel in his element when doing these roles. Sarastro in *Zauberflöte* and Commendatore in *Don Giovanni* require a really low "basso profundo."

Mozart presumably disliked contraltos, for he wrote no parts for low female voices. Instead, he required that his sopranos have an enormous range.

Mozart's operatic roles ask for great skill in ensemble singing. Two or three, and often as many as seven solo voices are required to join in the most demanding chamber music.

The typical Mozart singer sings as if he were a member of a string quartet where every one of the four players is, so to speak, part of one big instrument.

He conceives the music in a chamber-musical way, both when he sings solo together with the orchestra and in the ensemble with his fellow singers.

He never allows his own voice to dominate and outsing the rest of the ensemble.

He must be able to accomplish a light use of his voice. Of course, this does not mean that he has to sing *piano* all the time, but he must never allow his passion or voice power to overcome the consistent and equable quality of tone.

He must see to it that he has perfect control, not only of his own voice, but of the complete musical structure of the opera.

Exquisite recordings of all the more frequently performed Mozart operas are available, but the fine recordings from the first Fritz Busch Glyndebourne performances in 1939 still rate very high.

With its capacity of 433 people, the Glyndebourne Opera House in Ringmer, Sussex, England, lent the intimacy of a chamber performance to the Mozart operas, which made them close to ideal. No singer had to strain his voice to be heard. The orchestra consisted of thirty-three players, and the great artistry of Fritz Busch's uncompromising, warm, and vital conducting achieved a nearly perfect result. The singers had been picked from all over the world and stayed at the Glyndebourne estate, spending their time rehearsing Mozart in the beautiful surroundings of the Sussex Downs. Because of the enthusiasm and lavishness of Mr. John Christie—who had built the opera house as a private stage for his wife, Audrey Mildmay, the fine Mozart singer—these Mozart performances were almost a reproduction of the performances given at the princely courts of Mozart's own time.

GIOACCHINO ROSSINI (1792–1868), GAETANO DONIZETTI (1797–1848), VINCENZO BELLINI (1801–1835), and LUIGI CHERUBINI (1760–1842)

Virtuosity and technical acrobatics are the primary demands on the performers of the various roles of the Italian operas from the beginning of the nineteenth century.

Only when there are singers at hand who can master the trills, florid runs, and other embellishments is it possible to give a performance of these operas which is true to the original. In Rossini's *Il Barbiere di Siviglia* (The Barber of Seville), written in 1816, thirty years after Mozart's *Marriage of Figaro,* Rosina, Don Bartolo, and Figaro are the soul and spirit of one of the greatest comic operas ever written (listen to *Il Barbiere di Siviglia* conducted by Erich Leinsdorf, or to Alceo Galliera conducting, with Maria Callas, Tito Gobbi, and others.)

When an aria like "Una furtiva lagrima" from Donizetti's *L'Elisir d'amore* (The Elixir of Love), composed in 1832, is sung with its mixture of sweet Neapolitan folk song and the true bel canto of early Italian operas, it has the stamp of perfect vocalism (listen to Tito Schipa).

The singer whose renderings of arias from this period come closest to the ideal is Maria Callas. The embellishments, to her, mean genuine outbursts of the anger and despair of Norma's soul in Bellini's opera of the same name (1831). She manages to give "... the intensity of dramatization through the singing voice" that Paul Henry Lang praised in his *Music in Western Civilization.**

In Cherubini's *Medea,* Maria Callas's performance of the title role is a most striking demonstration of this. After the crisp and vital overture and great singing by fine Italian singers, her short first phrase, "Io? Medea!" has the effect of a heavy blow on the head in all its awesomeness and smoldering hatred (listen to both *Norma* and *Medea* conducted by Tullio Serafin).

LUDWIG VAN BEETHOVEN (1770–1827) and KARL MARIA VON WEBER (1786–1826)

The singer who wants to tackle the various parts of the two early German operas, Beethoven's *Fidelio* (1805) and Weber's *Der Freischütz* (The Free Shooter) (1821), must bear in mind the social and political background that caused their creation. *Fidelio* is based on the ideology of freedom from tyranny. It is a so-called rescue opera. Beethoven was involved in the revolutionary ideas of his time and sought to express these thoughts and emotions in his great music. The singers of Leonore's and Florestan's parts must have large and powerful voices to carry above the rich and loud orchestra. Beethoven didn't have much compassion or sympathy for vocal artists. (Listen to *Fidelio* with Otto Klemperer conducting, with Christa Ludwig, Jon Vickers, and others.)

Weber based the story of his opera on old German legends. He

* *Op. cit.*

tried to get completely free of the Italian style and way of interpretation and establish a genuinely German romantic atmosphere (listen to Lotte Lehmann as Agathe). Agathe is one of the principal characters, and her soprano arias—"Leise, leise fromme Weise" (Softly, Softly, Pious Song) and "Und ob die Wolke sich verhüllte" (Even If the Clouds Hid It)—stand as the operatic parallel of the Schubert Lieder in their true romantic melodiousness.

CHARLES GOUNOD (1818–1893), GEORGES BIZET (1838–1875), JULES MASSENET (1842–1912), and GIACOMO PUCCINI (1858–1924)

Instead of discussing the numerous grand operas of the nineteenth century, I shall attempt to give some typical examples of roles the singer can interpret in a truly dramatic way. Not only do most of the principal roles in these operas offer a wide scope for brilliant vocal display, but the singer has ample opportunity to lend them soul and body. You as the singer must study the libretto of the whole opera to be able to portray your role in the right relationship to the other roles. Often librettos are based on novels that inspired the composer, and in such a case it is a good idea to read the novel to understand the background of the work.

Gounod's *Faust* (1859), Bizet's *Carmen* (1875), and Massenet's *Manon* (1884) are all in what is called the "French" singing style, despite the fact that *Faust* is "German" and *Carmen* "Spanish." It is a matter of language. French words are placed differently in the resonance room than are Italian and German words. The French phrase "Salut, demeure chaste et pure" is sung with a voice totally unlike the voice that sings the corresponding line in Italian, "Salve, dimora casta e pura," or in German, "Gegrüsst sei mir, du keusche Stätte." The free and open vowel sounds of Italian and the cumbersome and guttural consonants of German produce phrases that are totally different in character and ambiance from that evoked by the French line. Another reason that these three operas are said to be in the "French" style is the elegant and subtle way the composers attempted to give a psychological explanation to the actions and motivations of their characters. This is characteristically French, and is encountered not only in French music but in French literature too, and indeed in the very approach to human relationships of the French people themselves.

The role of Marguerite in *Faust* should be learned by every lyric soprano. The famous "Jewel Song" is both a simple, sustained folk song and a coloratura part with dramatic leaps and runs. It is effective when sung with great elegance.

Faust sings the amorous cavatina, "Salut, demeure chaste et pure," a well-turned tenor aria with the much-desired high C, which secures the singer hundreds of tenor parts if he can render it in a free and convincing way. Mephistopheles is a true "actor-singer" part. Along with the demanding bass singing in "Le veau d'or" (The Golden Calf), both by the sound of evil in his voice and by his acting, he must give the listeners the eerie feeling that they are in the presence of Satan himself. (Listen to Feodor Chaliapin, the greatest and most satanic of them all, and to *Faust* conducted by André Cluytens with Victoria de los Angeles, Nicolai Gedda, Boris Christoff, and others.)

In *Carmen,* Bizet created a Spanish atmosphere, with Spanish dancing, Spanish rhythm, Spanish decor, toreadors, and bullfights, but the opera is still unmistakably French. Its catching, fiery music is known and loved by thousands outside music circles, and the show and plot are unusually well constructed. The tenor who sings the role of Don José must present a clear-cut and concise characterization of this jealous lover, who is driven to the insane killing of Carmen. She is a ruthless and superstitious gypsy, the female counterpart of Mozart's Don Giovanni, the great seducer. Wherever she goes, she attracts lovers, but she has great personal pride and is not just a common streetwalker. Only the singer who understands these characteristics of Carmen can possibly give a true portrayal of her. (Listen to Herbert von Karajan conducting, with Leontyne Price, Franco Corelli, Robert Merrill, Mirella Freni, and others.)

Massenet's *Manon* is based on Abbé Prévost's psychological study of the poor Chevalier Des Grieux, but little of his complex state of mind has been expressed in the opera, which concentrates on the unhappy fate of Manon. The plot is intricate and dramatic, and Massenet wrote soprano and tenor arias full of amorous abandon. While *Faust* has a German and *Carmen* a Spanish flavor, Massenet's opera is as French as it can be, in both story and music. It is next to impossible for the non-French singer to identify with the decadent life of the French nobility in the eighteenth century. Manon's aria "Adieu, notre petite table" is a touching good-bye to the short-lived happiness she enjoyed with Des Grieux in love and poverty, and in it she reveals her genuine feelings toward him. In the dream aria "En fermant les yeux," the tenor who can sustain a true *mezza voce* all the way through will accomplish the strongest effect by subdued and refined singing. The beautiful aria "Ah, fuyez, douce image" expresses his desperate struggle to forget the bewitching Manon. It is one of the most exacting arias in all of French grand opera. (Listen to Pierre Monteux conducting, with Victoria de los Angeles and others.)

To the enthusiastic but indiscriminate opera fan, Puccini's tuneful, yet sentimental and "syrupy" operas are the ideal. *La Bohème* (1896), with its description of the artists' and poets' life in the Latin Quarter of Paris in 1830 is everyone's favorite, but *Tosca* (1900), *Madame Butterfly* (1904), and *Turandot* (first performance in 1926, two years after Puccini's death) are also greatly loved. The open and concise vowels and the crisp and almost explosive consonants of the Italian language make it perfect for singing. The voice production is free and flowing in both spoken and sung Italian, and Puccini was a master at fitting his music to the spoken language. In the arias "Mi chiamano Mimi, ma il mio nome é Lucia" (They Call Me Mimi, But My Name Is Lucia) and "Quando m'en vo soletta per la via," you can safely follow Puccini's rhythmical pattern and indications as closely as in a Bach or a Handel recitative. Eschew portamenti, ritardandi, long holds, and other gimmicks of bad musical taste (even if some Italian singers do not). Puccini's music contains enough of these already. If you feel that the phrasing needs gliding from tone to tone, do it on the consonants and not on the vowels. "Mi chiamano Mimi" will serve as an example: not Mi chia-a-ma-a-no-o Mi-i-mi, but Mi chia-ma-no Mimi.

From "Che gelida manina," one of the best-known tenor arias in *La Bohème,* there is this typical phrase: "e i bei sogni miei" (and my beautiful dreams). In this aria, Puccini indicated the kind of portamento he wanted: *Con grande espressivo,* which does *not* mean scooping and gliding, but only very legato. (Listen to Thomas Schippers conducting, with Freni, Gedda, and others.)

Puccini is not too successful at psychological characterization. In *Madama Butterfly*, for example, Pinkerton, the American naval officer who deserts Butterfly, lacks personality; and Madama Butterfly herself has not much more Japanese about her than her costume and make-up. Both Pinkerton and Butterfly have some gorgeous arias, in which the sheer beautiful sound is intoxicating and overwhelming. (Listen to Santini conducting, with de los Angeles, Björling, and others.)

GIUSEPPE VERDI (1813–1901), RICHARD WAGNER (1813–1883), CLAUDE DEBUSSY (1862–1918), and RICHARD STRAUSS (1864–1949)

The two overshadowing names in nineteenth-century opera are Richard Wagner and Giuseppe Verdi. Despite their widely different expressions of thought and form, their works come closer to the original conception of a *dramma per musica* than any of the other nineteenth-century operas. Their approaches to the problems of opera are as divergent as the national characters of Italians and Germans. It is a matter of the taste and temperament of the interpreter whether to choose the human world of Verdi's operas or the superhuman mythological unreality of Wagner's. Both ask for enormous voices; Wagner, perhaps, more so, because the vocal sound has to stand out as a solo instrument above the huge Wagnerian orchestra.

Verdi relies more on vital acting and vocal brilliance. The Wagnerian concept of operatic singing, to pour out sound full blast for hours with little dramatic action, is more in accordance with the German-Teutonic mentality. With the lively Italians this does not agree; it simply goes against their grain.

In his extensive, ponderous, and often polemic writings, Wagner gave the performer minute instructions for interpreting various roles. He felt that a true understanding of dramatic psychology was of the greatest importance to the singer who wanted to portray the characters exactly the way he, Wagner, had created them. He had revolutionary ideas about the operatic genre and broke with traditional opera writing. He hailed the *Gesamtkunstwerk,* a complex of the various phases of dramatic art, poetry, music, and action. He protested against the absolute demand for "melody" which was so evident in all previous opera writing, and his aim was to make opera or musical drama a symphonic poem. The performer, he believed, should fully understand the deeper meaning and emotions in this "poem" before participating in a presentation of it. He maintained that this spiritual understanding might to some extent conquer the taxing physical demand his music made on the voice. The singer who is qualified to sing Wagnerian roles, and who has the vocal potential for them, should acquaint himself with Wagner's own uncompromising ideas of how they should be performed.

In the highly gifted singer Ludwig Schnorr, from the Dresden Opera, Wagner thought he had found the ideal performer for the heroic tenor roles he had created. The handsome young man, whose tenor voice was of rare beauty, understood and admired Wagner's music, and Wagner personally coached him, not only from the piano but also on the stage.

The following passage describes the painstaking method in which Wagner worked with a singer during a rehearsal of *Tannhäuser*:

> There . . . I took my stand, close by his side, and, following the music and surrounding scenic incidents bar by bar, . . . whispered him the inner cycle of the entranced's emotions, from the sublimest ecstasy of complete unconsciousness to the gradual wakening of his senses to their present environment, his ear being first to return to life—while, as if to shield the wonder from disturbance, he forbids his eye, now unchained from the magic spell of Heaven's ether, to look as yet upon the homely world of earth. The gaze fixed movelessly on high, merely the physiognomic play of features, and finally a gentle slackening of the body's rigid upright pose, betray the stir of gained rebirth; till every cramp dissolves beneath the whelming miracle, and he breaks down at last in humbleness, with the cry: "Almighty, to Thy name be praise! Great are

> the wonders of Thy grace!" Then, with the hushed share he takes in the pilgrims' chant, the look, the head, the whole posture of the kneeling man, sink even deeper; till choked with sobs, and in a second, saving swoon, he lies prone, unconscious, face to earth.*

Wagner's directions regarding the singer's emotional state, vocal emission, and stage behavior may seem intolerably meticulous, but he is an example of a composer who gives us an exact idea of the way he wants his work performed. The singer must be receptive to these directions, yet still preserve his own personality, for "without the interpreter's imagination, the score remains forever soulless, pen music—nothing more."†

Not only the full development of the voice but the physical growth of the body to its maturity is absolutely necessary to do justice to Wagner's highly demanding vocal parts. A forced and pinched voice is frequently heard when a young singer attempts to execute the sustained phrases of Wagner's music. The singer must not appear to be struggling to have his voice heard over the orchestral din. The typical Wagnerian voice may be compared to the weighty sound of the trombone; whereas in Mozart the singer uses a light clarinet or flutelike voice. Of course, there are high trumpetlike sounds in Wagner and low bassoonlike passages in Mozart's vocal music; but the typical Wagner voice is heavy, and the Mozart voice is light, this being one of the principal differences between the two operatic styles.

Verdi's many operas established him as Italy's greatest national composer. His operas offered the most striking contrast of approach to the music dramas of his German rival, Wagner. As Curt Sachs

* A. Goldman and E. Sprinchorn, *Wagner on Music and Drama: A Compendium of Richard Wagner's Prose Works* (New York: E. P. Dutton & Co., Inc., 1964), pp. 339–340.
† *Ibid.*, p. 283.

puts it, there is an "eternal antithesis between the playing North and the singing South."* The Italian is impatient to get to the essential thing right away, which to him means the singing.

The Italian audience is fast to acknowledge a free and sonorous vocal sound, but woe to the singer whose voice lacks a sunny sweetness and *slancio* (élan, throw), for he will bore them in spite of his musicianship and feeling for style. "We have barking dogs in Italy, too!" was one cruel Italian comment on the singing of a guest from abroad.

Only in his late operas did Verdi become interested in expressing the deeper motivations for his characters. In *Otello* (1887) and *Falstaff* (1892), he succeeded in bringing out the psychological content in the vocal line itself.

Falstaff is Verdi's last work and only comic opera. A long life of experience and success lay behind him, when, at the age of seventy-nine, nine years before his death, he wrote this work. Paul Henry Lang writes of it: "*Falstaff* is Verdi's bitterest exposure of life, yet it is also its most triumphal defense. With profound sorrow the aged composer unveils the tragic fate of a dreamer in the prosaic realities of life. Soul and character should be sketched by the drama, but they must be realized and rendered by the music."†

The role of Falstaff, the sly and roguish lover of women and wine, makes heavy demands, in both psychological singing and acting, and has been a challenge to operatic baritones ever since it was conceived. The baritone who sings the role must have a great sense of humor and a talent for projecting this in the numerous comic situations that occur (listen to Bernstein conducting, with Fischer-Dieskau and others).

Among the operatic creations that lead into our own time, Debussy's only opera, *Pelléas et Mélisande* (1902), uses the voice in

* "The Road to Major," *Musical Quarterly* 29 (1943):403.

† *Music in Western Civilization* (New York: W. W. Norton & Company, Inc., 1941), p. 912.

a new and original way. This opera does not contain a single "aria," but its declamatory singing in recitative style produces an intensely poetic mood which is closely connected to the French language. It would not be possible to express the nuances of the words and the often subconscious emotions in any other language (listen to Cluytens conducting, with de los Angeles, Jansen, and others).

Of the many operas by Richard Strauss, *Salome* (1905), *Elektra* (1909), and *Der Rosenkavalier* (1911) are the most important. Strauss was an excellent conductor and was able to bring out the numerous effects of the instruments in the orchestra with great virtuosity. He was deeply influenced by the revolutionary compositional ideas of Wagner. He managed, however, to create a style of his own, in which the sound of each instrument of the orchestra asserts itself. After the Biblical and classical Greek topics, *Salome* and *Elektra,* he played with the idea of writing an *opera buffa* à la Mozart. In close collaboration with the German poet Hugo von Hofmannsthal, he composed *Der Rosenkavalier,* which is regarded by many as his most significant opera. Here Strauss turned to the ideas of the pre-Wagnerian period and gave priority to the voice in a refined interplay with the orchestra. *Der Rosenkavalier* certainly contains all the ingredients of, say, *Le Nozze di Figaro.* The mature and passionate singing of the Marschallin, who is deserted by her husband and has a love affair with the seventeen-year-old Count Octavian, has the same flavor as the singing of the Countess Almaviva to young Cherubino. Although I find it slightly distasteful, the lover, Octavian, is—like Cherubino—a so-called trouser role, a woman "disguised" as a man.

A similar parallel exists between Sophie from *Der Rosenkavalier* and Susanna from *Figaro.* Far from being an imitation, either in character or in singing, *Der Rosenkavalier* is a wonderful mixture of a Mozart opera and a Johann Strauss operetta. The parallel to the Mozart roles is actually weak; Richard Strauss had no intention of remodeling any particular Mozart opera, but the wit, elegance, and charm of both Mozart and Johann Strauss are evident in *Der*

Rosenkavalier. Therefore the singer should bear in mind that the time and world of *Der Rosenkavalier* is that of Mozart and the Austrian Empress Marie-Thérèse right after the middle of the eighteenth century (listen to Karajan conducting, with Schwarzkopf, Ludwig, Edelmann, and others).

Such twentieth-century operas as Maurice Ravel's *L'Heure Espagnole* (1911), Darius Milhaud's *Le Boeuf sur le toit,* Alban Berg's *Wozzeck* (1921) and *Lulu* (1928–1934), Benjamin Britten's *Peter Grimes* (1945), *The Rape of Lucretia* (1946), and *Albert Herring* (1948), Gian Carlo Menotti's *The Medium* (1947) and *The Consul* (1950), Igor Stravinsky's *The Rake's Progress* (1951), Francis Poulenc's *Dialogues des Carmelites* (1953) and *Les Mamelles de Tirésias* (1940), Karl-Birger Blomdahl's *Aniara* (1959), Samuel Barber's *Antony and Cleopatra* (1966) indicate the enormous vitality and growth of operatic composition. This is a field lying wide open for the modern-minded opera singer.

Paul Henry Lang has this to say about the future of opera:

> As long as men will jubilate in their happiness and laugh and sing, as long as they will cry and shout in the agony of pain and unhappiness, opera will be appreciated because opera endeavors not to render the panorama of life, but to give life itself, to depict man as he is, in the realm of passions that are intangible or inexpressible in mere words.*

* *Ibid.*, p. 331.

V

Teacher, Coach, and Accompanist

Many times, beginning singers have asked me which voice teacher I would recommend for them. The question is a bit awkward, as one can't answer, "Me, of course!" and one doesn't always want to, either. It is, however, a perfectly understandable inquiry, and my answer is always, "You will have to run the risk and take the responsibility yourself," a response that will give both student and teacher a fair chance.

A teacher may be wonderful for one student and have a bad effect on the voice of another one. You may have asked your fellow students where to seek the teacher who will be best for you. "Don't go to that one, he forces the voice," one friend warns. "Go to this one, he is kind and understanding." Perhaps you follow this advice only to find that your "choice" pushes your voice so that it hurts and does not understand your specific problems at all. The opposite case is just as common. In the long run you may have to find the teacher for you by the trial-and-error method, but the following pieces of advice may serve to guide you:

1. Go with an open mind and a perfect willingness to follow the instructions of your teacher as best you can.

2. Try to understand his corrections. If they seem obscure, ask him to clarify them.

3. From the very first lesson, work with a tape recorder when you practice. What you hear inside your head is totally different from the auditory picture your teacher and the tape recorder get.

4. In most cases the teacher will try to establish a good, friendly atmosphere. Without your cooperation this cannot be done.

5. From the very first scale or exercise you do, remember that you are producing sound in order to catch the interest of an audience. Don't sing to your teacher, or to the person at the piano, or to the floor. Always sing out to an imaginary group of listeners who are anxious to receive what you give them. The teacher will prove to be a good one for you if he is able to guide your "out-going" efforts.

In your efforts to follow his guidance you may stiffen and get tense. Try to relax. A relaxed and comfortable atmosphere is the only one in which the voice can develop. If, after a half or a whole year's conscientious work with a teacher, you feel that for some reason you are not benefiting vocally, ask your teacher to excuse you, and try another teacher. The wise voice teacher will realize that the main basis for his instruction, *confidence,* has been lost, but he will also realize that your voice belongs to you alone, and *you* have to see to it that it is not ruined or irreparably damaged. In my experience it has been very advantageous to my singing to change teachers, and I am all for it, even if it may cause disappointment for the teacher at first.

If the singer wants advice in addition to the information that he has already received from his teacher, he will have to obtain a *coach.* The coach's function is to make the singer ready for his performance in all respects. In his excellent book *The Art of Accompanying and Coaching,** Kurt Adler gives extensive advice and suggestions about the important role of the coach.

It is not a good idea to have your voice teacher accompany you at recitals, however good a pianist he may be, and the coach, too, should refrain from acting as your accompanist. Both the coach and the teacher are too involved in your various vocal and musical problems. The ideal situation is that you be as well prepared as possible by the voice teacher and the coach, and then, after thorough rehearsal, do the performance with an *assisting artist.*

* Minneapolis: University of Minnesota Press, 1965.

When the singer is finally ready to join "the other instrument," he will, in most cases, feel that he is being supported and that his preliminary work is bringing results. He will feel perhaps like the little vine that finally grows large enough to need a trellis to support it.

Many singers think that the first thing they want from an accompanist is his ability to "follow" them. Actually, the reverse is true. The singer must feel free in his phrasing and sure of his support, but the accompanist must keep him to the tempo and to the whole pattern of the music. This is why it is absolutely necessary from the very beginning to have a first-rate accompanist. By no means accompany yourself. If you do, you will overindulge your vocal phrasing. Besides, you will have to concentrate at least 50 per cent of your time on piano playing, and you need all 100 per cent for your singing.

You need help in your efforts to recreate the work of art the poet and composer created. If you have an unrhythmical and inhibited pianist fumbling with his own notes, you will invariably receive and, in turn, pass on to the audience a misleading conception of the composition. Look for an accompanist who is so superior a pianist that he can handle not only his own phrases but yours, too, and make a unity of the two. He must "sing" your phrases—not aloud, of course, but to himself. It is essential that the accompanist feel the phrasing vocally. He must actually breathe along with the singer.

Long ago, the outstanding Danish accompanist Anker Blyme and I sang in the Copenhagen Boys Choir. Later, when accompanying me, he often became so absorbed in the total content of the song that he would forget himself and hum audibly. Many times I had to tell him: "Tonight *I* sing, and *you* do the playing only!"

In my singing career I have had the good fortune to be assisted by the very finest accompanists. Herman D. Koppel is not only a marvelous pianist and accompanist, but a composer and one of

Denmark's finest musicians. In addition to his technical and musical abilities, he possesses something that you can only hope your assisting artist has: a true human understanding! After my surgery, he was fully aware of my problems and supported my efforts to regain some of the vocal qualities I had lost. The sounds I produced after my illness were not the same as they had been earlier, when he accompanied me in nine performances in a row of the Schubert cycle *Die schöne Müllerin.* But during my long, slow recovery he supported me with the incredible patience and love of the true friend.

Two other excellent pianists with whom I have worked are Gerald Moore, "the unashamed accompanist," now retired, and the late Paul Ulanowsky, the brilliant and refined chamber musician of the famous Bach Aria Group. Both of these men were fully aware of the important role of the accompanist, and at the same time both were intent on presenting the total musical picture of voice and piano. Both knew a lot about the various vocal problems they had encountered and had to put up with, but they never gave any unsolicited and unwanted suggestions regarding the singer's technique. Of course, both commented many times on my interpretation of a particular song, but only as far as the musical aspect was concerned.

Inspiration is a haggard word, but you will receive inspiration, that divine spark, from your "assistant at the piano" only if you have the greatest respect for his work. The two artists must always feel absolutely free to make suggestions to each other and to make any criticism that may benefit their mutual efforts. Of course, just as the accompanist should respect the singer's craft, the singer should never tell his accompanist how to do his finger work or pedaling. "Friendly guidance" of this type invariably leads to discord and a poor relationship.

Both Moore and Ulanowsky adhered to the famous words of Schubert: "The manner and way in which Vogl sings and I accompany, in which at such a moment *we seem to be one,* is something quite new to these people." And both agreed with Schumann that

"The voice cannot reproduce everything or produce every effect; together with the expression of the whole, the finer details should also be expressed—that is, by the accompanying instrument."

It was a great privilege to make music with these two men, both of whom helped me form my whole idea of Lieder singing. I always looked forward to my sessions with Gerald Moore, with all his exuberant vitality and fun. "That was not bad, *for us*!" he said once with a grin, when we listened to a playback of one of our recordings. I am so vain as to believe he enjoyed it, too. And once, Ulanowsky, during those horrible moments just before we went on stage, said, "Now, Aksel, let's go in and *improvise*!" We were about to do Schubert's *Winterreise* in the National Gallery in Washington, D.C. Improvisation in the usual sense of the word was not exactly the right word after all the rehearsing we had done; but in the very act of recreating the musical work, this is actually what should take place, for the true artist never does a piece of music quite the same way twice.

The singer who has made it "to the front row" must always see to it that he gets an accompanist of the finest quality, not only because he owes it to himself but also because he owes it to his audience. Too often you hear great singers with mediocre accompanists. A second-rate accompanist may save the singer money, but in the long run it is most assuredly detrimental to the artistic result.

That Lieder singing is chamber music, a duet between two instruments, one of which is the human voice, is best illustrated by Gerald Moore in his book *The Unashamed Accompanist,* which has become a classic. "The partnership between singer and accompanist," he says, "is a fifty-fifty affair." And later: "The first page of Schubert's 'Im Frühling' (In Springtime) from which the following example is taken, is a good song to practise in this way, making the soprano voice in the piano part sing. And we should make it our aim to sing as sweetly as he [the singer]."*

* London: Ascherberg, 1964, pp. 26–27.

In *Am I Too Loud?*, Gerald Moore said about his collaboration with John Coates, the English singer, "He taught me all I know about accompanying."* This statement is a striking example of Gerald Moore's readiness to work with the singer as a team. All singers should read his books, especially *The Unashamed Accompanist.*

* New York: The Macmillan Company, 1963, p. 29.

VI
The Recital

From your very first technical work with your voice, it should always be your aim to project not only the sound but also your personality. Not for one single moment, however, may you forget that the sole justification for being a singer is to let your voice be the medium for the message of beauty that you want to convey to your listeners.

While he is still under the supervision of his teacher, the student should do some performing, either for other students (who are severe critics!) or for private audiences. Gradually he must try to stand on his own feet and give a performance that expresses his individual personality—not somebody else's. He must develop a sense of responsibility toward his own musical intuitions, free from the influences of, for instance, his teacher. Of course, he will put into use what he has learned through his years of study, but the *art of performance* is to a great extent something he has to acquire through experience. As long as the young singer is strongly attached to his teacher (or to the "knitting club," that atrocious and sentimental phenomenon consisting of teacher, fellow students, sweetheart, parents, aunts, and other relations), he is not ready to begin performing. He must cut the umbilical cord that binds him to this coterie in order to become an independent performing artist. This does not mean that he should eschew advice and suggestions, but he should have matured enough to be able to listen critically and objectively to them, and he should be able to criticize himself.

It is hard to decide when the right moment has arrived for having someone handle the commercial side of your future career. Before a manager or impresario will gamble on you, he will expect you to have had past personal success, and he will want to ascertain that there is public demand for your talents. Impresarios are usually not philanthropists, but some of them are wise and music-loving persons who will guide your career and help you to make a living with your art.

Most musical artists complain that their impresarios do nothing for them. In most cases this is not a fair statement. If you are a success with your audiences, you need not worry; the impresario will have no difficulty selling you.

The part of your fee that you pay to your manager, impresario, or agent is well worth it, since artists are not the best merchants of their own goods. The singer cannot very well tell his "customers" how exceptional and brilliant he is. Someone else has to recommend him, and this the impresario is well equipped to do.

PROGRAMMING

The traditional arrangement of a recital may seem a little incongruous today. There are so many imponderabilia involved that it is hard to give a recipe for the proceedings. You may want to adjust your program to the acoustics of the hall, the instrument, the assisting artist, or the audience, since you cannot assume that all of these factors are ideal. The important thing, however, is that for a couple of hours you have to keep your audience voluntarily captive, whatever the conditions. A well-constructed program is the best fare you can offer.

Assembling a recital program is one of the most demanding chores in a career of performing. It involves much more than just sitting down at your desk and suggesting a group of this and a group of that from your repertoire. You will have to visualize or "audioize" your presentation of the various songs and, as far as possible, the reaction of the audience. To what extent will you be able to convey to them the intentions of the composer and poet?

No artist wants to feel bound to a fixed outline, which often results in a boring and too conventional kind of program anyway, nor is a chronological structure necessary or desirable.

A recital program should be well rounded and interestingly varied; it should contain both light and heavy music. Include some easily digested pieces; a menu does not consist of steak exclusively. Your artistry can be demonstrated equally well in both types of music. Your program might include four or five groups of songs. I suggest three before and two after the intermission. The opening group may consist of songs from any period, as long as they are melodious and not too complicated. The first song of the entire program should be lively, easy, and not too long, not only because you need such a song to fight stage fright but also to give the audience a chance to get accustomed to your whole appearance.

The second or third group could comprise compositions that are the most stimulating intellectually, both for you and for the listeners. These might be some lesser known pieces or even a first performance of contemporary music.

A light and gay, at best a familiar, group of songs should follow, and then the intermission, which I definitely think should be included in every program. The intermission gives your audience a chance to relax, to stretch their legs, perhaps to smoke, and to discuss what they have been hearing. Thus refreshed, they may be interested in a group of lesser-known songs. This is the moment to serve them a novelty.

End the program with another group of easily digested songs. In English-speaking countries, these should definitely be in English. Never work your audience too hard. Your recital must reveal the different sides of your talent and temperament; only then will you have that wonderful experience of holding your audience "in the hollow of your hand."

One of the most serious mistakes is to plan a program that lasts too long. Remember, "I wish he had sung some more!" is a better reaction than "Oh, my, wasn't it a long affair?"

As to encores, you have to play it by ear, but here I suggest that even if people should applaud enthusiastically, don't let yourself be tempted to sing too many "extras."

If you choose to perform a cycle, your program is a special one, and in many respects a more rewarding one, for you can stay in one world of imagery, adhere to the feelings of one person, and interpret one poetic idea in a continuous musical setting.

If you choose Schubert's *Winterreise*, the ideal thing musically and artistically is that it be sung nonstop. Practically, though, I think few audiences are able to digest those twenty-four expressions of despair, jealousy, sorrow, and even insanity without an intermission or some kind of break. A cycle is composed as a unit, and the last song is the end of it. It would be irreverent and wrong to add an encore just to please the audience.

It is also wrong to include operatic arias in a recital program. Opera should be acted, but the recital stage is not the place for acting. Leporello's aria "Madamina, il catalogo è questo" (Little Lady, This Is the List) sung without acting, in white tie and tails, is a ridiculous monstrosity. The singing of an art song on the concert stage is a dramatic event in itself, and "acting" the song is improper if the singer is to interpret it as Schubert, Debussy, or Sibelius wished it to be interpreted. The operatic singer inevitably feels inhibited if he is not allowed to act. Nevertheless, he has a peculiar urge to go on recital tour and sing his arias on the concert stage. The audience who goes to hear an operatic "name" thus often gets the wrong impression of a song recital, which in its pure and intimate form is becoming rare.

"No trumpets—only Dad singing?" was once the disappointed remark of one of my children. I am sorry to say that this attitude is common with the adult musical public, too. "Artist Series" and similar concert institutions must take the blame for the frequent mishmash programs offered to the public. These often consist of a bouquet of operatic arias, Negro spirituals done in a cheap theatrical style (these should rather be sung by Negro congregations and certainly not from the concert stage), and a few songs from popular musical comedies. The three main categories of song—the art song, the oratorio, and the opera—must be kept separate. Their true homes are, respectively, the recital hall, the church, and the theater or opera house.

TRANSLATIONS

The problem of presenting art songs, oratorios, and operas in the original language is often the subject of heated and subjective discussions.

Look at it from the point of view of the audience, rather than from that of the performers.

I would definitely translate oratorio and opera into the language of the country in which they are performed. The purpose in both cases is to reach a large number of people. In opera—the sung play—the plot must be clearly understood by everybody, and any foreign language is bound to prevent this.

Wagner's *Lohengrin,* Verdi's *Aida,* and Bizet's *Carmen* undoubtedly reach their highest artistic value when sung in the original, but the sacrifice of translation has to be made to obtain that close connection between the action on stage and an audience that is of a different nationality from the librettist.

It happens often that a guest artist from a foreign country sings the star role in a translated opera. Then you might run into somewhat confusing situations when you hear in Italian and German: "Will you meet me at midnight?" and the answer is "Yes, at five it will be!" I don't think such a Babel of tongues is common today, though.

It is still more urgent that oratorios be done in the language completely familiar to the listeners. Just as the Bible has been translated into every language, Handel's *Messiah,* Bach's *St. Matthew Passion,* and César Franck's *Les Béatitudes* only create the intimacy and true religious experience when sung in the vernacular.

As to the art song, the situation is somewhat different. To English-speaking people, it is perhaps not so awkward to hear Schubert's "Das Wandern ist des Müllers Lust" with the English words, "To Wander Is the Miller's Joy," but the musical values of the song are actually deteriorated that way. Short program notes give the idea of the contents. All German Lieder should be sung with German words, and the French mélodies should be sung in French, as they would lose too much if sung in English translation.

Only if the texts of the songs in question are prohibitive for the singer and the music is of such high quality that he feels he must perform them (e.g., Musorgski, Sibelius, Grieg, Carl Nielsen, etc.), should the singer follow the principle of having them translated into English.

Benjamin Britten said in his Aspen speech: "It is *insulting* to address anyone in a language that he does not understand." Still, it is a wise thought presented by Robert Frost: "Poetry is something which is lost in translation."

DICTION

The foreigner or "alien immigrant" living in America acquires his second language, English, in a way quite different from the way he learned his mother tongue. He learns it with the help of phonetics, the science of speech sounds. Because of this, he may become more "sound conscious" than the average native American, more aware of the sounds in his adopted language. Actually, the more concerned he is about imitating the sounds (and disregarding the spelling), the better his pronunciation will become. To be able to get the true sound of a foreign language is not, as is generally believed, a matter of musicality or a "musical ear." Many highly musical singers speak foreign languages with very heavy accents.

It is, rather, a matter of abstracting from your mother tongue and imitating the sounds of the other language.

If a foreigner is given an opportunity to teach diction phonetically, to tell his students how they should pronounce their own language, he is bound to be met with skepticism. (How would *he* know, poor foreigner?) Yet Benjamin Britten wanted his *Ceremony of Carols* to be recorded by the Copenhagen Boys Choir. The Danish boys have only a smattering of English, and there are hundreds of fine boys' choirs in England. However, through Britten's personal guidance, and by phonetic imitation of his words, the Danes managed to record with very clear diction.

Before you make any attempts to sing in a foreign language, however, you must make sure that you are able to articulate your own language properly. You must be aware of the positions of the articulating organs when you form the various sounds. A few simple songs in English that allow you to concentrate on the clear and definite enunciation of the various sounds are "O, Waly, Waly," "The Ash Grove," "Go from My Window, Go," "Greensleeves," and "O, No, John."

A thorough knowledge of the I.P.A. (International Phonetic Association) sound symbols is very helpful in enabling you to place the vowels and consonants of most Western languages properly. Most dictionaries use the I.P.A. symbols in their phonetic transcriptions. The dictionary, of course, does not supply the audible sounds themselves; for these you have to listen closely to the foreign language as spoken by a native, and then *imitate*. (A list of the I.P.A. symbols appears in Appendix I.)

The singer should know at least three languages in addition to his own, preferably Italian, German, and French. For a singer to *know* a language does not necessarily mean that he has to be able to speak it fluently. It *does* mean that he must know how to pronounce it correctly, and he must have some knowledge of its structure. The information he can obtain from a dictionary may lead him into terrible misunderstandings.

He must know not only the exact pronunciation and translation of every word he sings but also the intrinsic meaning of the simplest phrases. If he does not, he will not be able to recreate the poetic atmosphere the composer intended. The good composer makes every effort to fit his music not only to the words but also to the colors of the various vowel sounds and to the expressiveness of the consonants. The ideal way for the singer to fulfill the intentions of both poet and composer is to use the original sounds and poetic phrases.

ITALIAN

The Italian language is articulated with more energy than the English language is. The vowels are clean, pure, and uncompromising. An *a* is an [ɑ] and a *u* is a [u]. In English, *a* and *u* have at least three different sounds each.

In Italian the consonants are not a necessary evil that chop up the legato vocal line, but rather a wonderful help to the singer in his efforts to project. A characteristic of Italian pronunciation is that double consonants are always long.

In order to get the true accent or "throw" of the Italian language, the singer should, ideally, spend a year or so in Italy. Only the few lucky ones are able to do this. There are, however, many excellent recordings of spoken Italian which stress the very best pronunciation.

In Italian the spoken word is very close to the sung word. The Italian sings when he speaks! (The Tuscan dialect spoken north of Rome—Florence and environs—is regarded as the "best" Italian.)

For any singer, particularly if he wants an intimate knowledge of the rich operatic literature, it is absolutely necessary that he not only know how to *pronounce* Italian but also how to *sing* the language as well. He has to be familiar with the Italian operas of Mozart (*Don Giovanni*, *Le Nozze di Figaro*, and *Così fan tutte*) and with the operas of Donizetti, Rossini, Puccini, Verdi, Mascagni, and Leoncavallo, in the original language. If he then has to sing them in English, German, French, Finnish, Swedish, or even Danish, that is a practical question; but he has an obligation to know the original.

The Italian songs from the sixteenth and seventeenth centuries that are mentioned on page 6 are simple and appropriate for training in Italian diction. Many more could be found in *La Flora,** an excellent collection of songs in their original forms, with short translations and information about the composers.

GERMAN

The German and English languages belong to the same family, and many words have the same roots. This fact causes a great deal of confusion, not concerning the meaning, but concerning the pronunciation. The English word "land" [læ:nd] and the German word "Land" [lɑnt], for example, look alike and mean the same thing; but the English word has a long [æ] and a voiced final [d], and the German has a short [ɑ], a long [n], and a final [t].

Next to the Italians, I know of few peoples other than the Germans who take such natural joy in singing. It is second nature to the average German to express himself in song. This is equally true of the musically gifted German. Some of Mozart's operas, *Die Entführung aus dem Serail* and *Die Zauberflöte,* for example, and Bach's cantatas and Passions were written to German texts. The songs of Schubert, Schumann, Brahms, Wolf, Mahler, and Strauss were set to the words of great German poets: Goethe, Heine, Rückert, Mörike, Eichendorff, and many others.

German is sometimes regarded as difficult to sing, and it is true that there is one guttural sound in German: the *ch* [x] after *a, o,* and *u.* The corresponding voiced sound [R], as in "ruhen," as used in spoken language, is almost always substituted by [r] in singing. To avoid losing all the poetic atmosphere that lies in the German

* Knud Jeppesen, ed., Vols. 1–3 (Copenhagen: Wilhelm Hansen, 1949).

words and sounds, the singer has an obligation to learn the correct pronunciation.

In 1928, Theodor Siebs wrote a book on High German, *Deutsche Hochsprache,** "Bühnenaussprache" (Stage German), that is still regarded as the last word on German pronunciation. It has been revised and now contains a list of the most common German words with their I.P.A. transcriptions.

The most common problems and difficulties in learning German diction seem to be as follows:

1. *Double vowels* are long: "Aal" [ɑ:l] (eel,) "Speer" [ʃpe:r] (spear), "Boot" [bo:t] (boat); or *vowels followed by h* as in "lahm" [lɑ:m] (lame), "mehr" [me:r] (more), "Bohne" [bo:n] (bean), "Schuh" [ʃu:] (shoe), "Ähre" [ɛ:ʀə] (ear of corn or wheat), "Söhne" [zø:ne] (sons), "kühl" [ky:l] (cool); or the *vowel i when followed by an e* as in "hier" [hi:ʀ] (here); or *vowels followed by a single consonant* as in "Tag" [tɑ:ĸ] (day); or *vowels in "open" syllables* (syllables ending in vowel) as in "lesen" [le:zen] (read).

Vowels followed by double consonants are short: "Sommer" [zɔmə] (summer); or *vowels followed by consonant* clusters, "Land" [lɑnt] or "Asche" [aʃə] (ashes).

2. In the English language, [e], [ø], and [o] do not exist, therefore causing some difficulty in articulation. An aid in obtaining the right sound is to pronounce [i] and pronounce [ɛ] and then stop. the jaw halfway in its slow movement down from [i] to [ɛ]. This should produce [e]. Stopping the jaw halfway between (ɥ) and [œ] should produce [ø]. Stopping the jaw halfway between [u] and [ɔ] should produce [o].

3. The letter *l* is pronounced in Italian, German, and French with the tip of the flat tongue against the upper front teeth or just behind them. The English *l* is pronounced with the whole rim of the spoon-shaped tongue against the gum, which gives it a hollow, "vowelish" sound.

4. At the beginning of words *s* is voiced [z], when followed by

* Berlin: Gruyter & Co., 1961.

a vowel, as in "sehen" [ze:ən] (see), between two vowels as in "Rose" [ro:zə] (rose), and between a vowel and a voiced consonant as in "Gänse" [gɛnzə] (geese).

5. At the beginning of words *s* followed by *p* or *t* is pronounced [ʃ] as in "sparen" [ʃpa:ʀən] (spare) and "Stern" [ʃtɛʀn] (star), but not inside words, as in "Fenster" [fɛnstər] (window).

6. In German and English *z* stands for a different sound. The German pronunciation is [ts] (unvoiced).

7. That *ie* is [i:] and *ei* is [ɑɪ] can be remembered by using the English pronunciation of the *last* sound of the diphthong.

8. The *ch* is pronounced [x] after *a* as in "ach" [ɑx] (oh), and *o* as in "hoch" [ho:x] (high), and after *u* as in "Fluch" [flu:x] (curse). After *ä, ch* is pronounced [ç] as in "mächtig" [mɛçtiç] (mighty), after *e* as in "rechnen" [ʀɛçnən] (reckon), after *i* as in "ich" [iç] (I), after *ö* as in "möchte" [mœçtə] (might), after *ü* as in "Bücher" [byçə] (books), after *l* as in "Milch" [milç] (milk), after *n* as in "mancher" [mançə] (many a one), and after *r* as in "durch" [durç] (through). The letter *x* is a guttural sound made with the uvula against the tongue. It is not unlike gargling, but voiceless. The [ç] is similar to the beginning sound in "young" [jʌŋ], but voiceless.

9. When a German word starts with a vowel, a slight glottal stop should be heard. The final consonant of the previous word should never be carried over as it is in English. If the previous word ends with another vowel, there must be a hiatus between the two words.

10. Often German words consist of prefix, root, ending, and suffix, e.g., "unwissenschaftliches" (unscientific) or "Zueignung" (dedication). Combinations of words may result in one big terrifying word, e.g., "Geschirrspühlmaschinereinigungsmittel" (dishwasher detergent). You simply have to break them up into syllables [ʊn-vi-sen-ʃaft-liç] [tsu-aik-nʊŋ], and [gə-ʃɪʀ-ʃpy:l-ma-ʃi:nə-rai-nɪ-gʊŋs-mɪ-təl].

11. The final consonants not only of words but also of every single syllable have to be audible and concise.

Practice German diction by singing the simpler songs of Schubert and the following folk songs and popular songs: "In einem kühlen Grunde," "Lorelei" (poetry by Silcher), "Das Wandern" (Müller), "Heidenröslein" (Goethe), and "Wanderers Nachtlied (Der du von dem Himmel bist)" (Goethe).

FRENCH

Both in opera and in the art song, there is a big repertoire in French that is fascinating, both musically and artistically. French music must be sung in the original language. It is very difficult for non-French singers to acquire the previously discussed "French" singing style. They must first learn the exact pronunciation of the French words.

As in other languages, there are many dialects in French, but the dialect that is considered best is the one spoken in Tours and its environs. There are also differences in spoken and sung French. The most characteristic feature in French is the nasalized pronunciation of several vowels in certain combinations. This nasalization should never be overdone in singing. If you listen to the great French singers Charles Panzéra, Pierre Bernac, and Gérard Souzay, you will hear very little of that nasal sound; still it is there, and all three sing a beautiful and clearly articulated text.

The French vowel sounds are pretty much the same as in Italian except that the *i* is always [i] as in "affiche" [afiʃ] (poster) and never modified to [ɪ] as in the German "Fisch" or the English "fish" [fɪʃ].

French vowels are nasalized when followed by an *m* or *n*, as in "lampe" [lɑ̃:p] (lamp), "Jean" [ʒɑ̃] (John), "enfant" [ɑ̃fɑ̃] (child), "membre" [mɑ̃bʀ] (member), "fin" [fɛ̃] (end), "timbre" [tɛ̃bʀ] (timbre), "faim" [fɛ̃] (hunger), "pain" [pɛ̃] (bread), "Rheims" [ʀɛ̃s] (Rheims), "sein" [sɛ̃] (breast), "symbole" [sɛ̃bɔl] (symbol), "lyncher" [lɛ̃ʃe] (lynch), "nom" [nɔ̃] (name), "non" [nɔ̃] (no), "humble" [œ̃bl] (humble), and "brun" [bʀœ̃] (brown).

If the *m* and *n* are followed by another vowel, there is no nasalization, as in "amour" [amu:ʀ] (love) and "finir" [finiʀ] (finish). If the *m* and *n* are doubled, there is usually no nasalization: "sommeil" [sɔmɛj] (sleep), "donner" [dɔne] (give), but there are exceptions: "ennui" [ɑ̃nɥi] (boredom).

French orthographic diphthongs form one vowel sound as in "quai" [ke], "mais" [mɛ], "autre" [o:tʀ], "Paul" [pɔl], "reine" [ʀɛ:n], "deux" [dø], "neuf" [nœf], and "nous" [nu].

Some French consonants differ in their pronunciation from the English ones: ç [ç] as in "ça" [sa], *ch* [ʃ] as in "chaise" [ʃɛ:z], *g* [ʒ] as in "rouge" [ʀu:ʒ], *h* is often silent, though in some words you hear a weak aspiration as in "haine" [(h)ɛ:n], *j* [ʒ] as in "jardin" [ʒaʀdɛ̃], *l* [l] as in "salle" [sal] (same pronunciation as in Italian and German), *ll* [j] after *i* as in "famille" [famij]. *M* and *n* are silent when a preceding vowel is nasalized, *r* [ʀ] as "riche" [ʀiʃ] (or [r], which is generally used in singing), *x* [s] as in "dix" [dis], *gn* [ɲ] as in "champagne" [ʃɑ̃paɲ], *ti* [sj] as in "nation" [nasjõ], and *the* [t] as in "théâtre" [teatʀ].

A characteristic of the pronunciation of French is the liaison—the linking of words as in: "Il est un autre heureux amant" [i-lɛ-tœ̃-no:tʀœ-ʀø-za-mɑ̃]. This sentence is pronounced almost as if it were one long word with stress on every syllable, the last seven syllables *beginning with a consonant*.

There are three accents in French: the *accent aigu*, [ʹ] (acute accent); the *accent grave* [ˋ] (grave accent); and the *accent circonflexe*, [ˆ] (circumflex accent). These are orthographic signs and determine the color or quality of the vowel and sometimes make a difference in meaning, as in "ou" [u] (or) with no accent, and "où" [u] (where) with an *accent grave*.

Most final French consonants are silent, but sometimes *c*, *f*, *l*, and *r* are pronounced, as in "avec" [avɛk] (with), "boeuf" [bœf] (ox), "minéral" [mineral] (mineral), and "hier"[*j*ɛʀ] (yesterday).

The articulation and syllabification of the French language, like that of Italian, is much more definite and energetic (or intense) than that of English, and it is up to the singer to keep the proper balance between the clear and almost elaborate articulation of the text and the legato of the vocal line so characteristic of French song. The *bergerettes* of the eighteenth century are excellent for perfecting your French diction. Try practicing with "Maman, dites moi," "Menuet d'Exaudet," "Philis, plus avare que tendre," and "Lisette."

THE PERFORMANCE

It is an excellent principle to remain as normal as possible on the day of performance. Try not to work yourself into a state of nervous hysteria that wears you out before you walk on stage. You will need your energy for your performance. Take it easy, be lazy, but don't sleep all day long. You may find that you fully awaken only in the middle of your program, and that is too late!

Two experienced old singers once advised me to have a "quickie" either of cognac or acquavit five minutes before I walked on stage. I warn every performer against that. This habit will inevitably play tricks on you sooner or later in your program. Eat lightly, but not too near performance time. It is a terrible experience to feel hunger pangs in the middle of your singing, but it is just as bad to feel the pains of indigestion.

The track star who overtrains discovers, when the moment comes to make his record run, that he is too exhausted to do his very best. In the same way, the foolish singer who vocalizes extensively on the day of his performance, or even rehearses his entire program, may find that he is unable to bring out his voice at its best when he is finally "under fire."

It is a well-known fact that the hall in which you are to sing is part of your instrument. Before you give your recital, you must become familiar with it, even though it is empty. The resonance of the hall will always change either for the better or for the worse when there are people in it, but still it is important for you to get acquainted with it. Only the "third man" can truly judge the balance between accompaniment and voice. As objectively as possible, and from various spots in the hall, this third person should tell the performers if either of them is too loud or too soft. A singer colleague may inevitably say that the piano is too loud, and a friend of the accompanist may say that you can barely hear the piano. It is best, then, to choose a person who is just a music lover. We performers could not do without this specimen.

The moment has arrived, and it should be a moment of relief after all the excitement and anticipation. The lights in the hall are lowered, and those on the stage are raised. The spotlight is on *you.* There must be enough light for the audience to read the program and the notes. The notes should not contain full translations of the songs in foreign languages, but only the gist of the poem. If the program notes are too long, you will have finished the song before they have read the text. After all, the idea is that they should be able to enjoy your singing.

The dimming of the hall lights is your cue to enter. Your attitude should be one of happiness and gratification that so many people want to hear you perform. Through all the recital, but especially at your first entrance, it is essential to the success of your performance that you appear natural and genuine in your demeanor. Do not *run* onto the stage. Walk with dignity, even if the piano seems miles away.

Acknowledge, together with your assisting artist, the kind welcome of the audience. *Never forget that you are a team.* Take your time starting. Both you and the audience need a minute of relaxation. Applause is a wonderful stimulation, though it has a tendency to interrupt the construction of your program. (I wish it could become a tradition to have applause only after a full group.) When performing a cycle, the singer can prevent any disturbing applause after the individual songs either by his expression concentrating on the next song or by discreetly waving off any spontaneous clapping.

Insist on having the doors closed while you are singing. It is distracting for the singer and especially for the audience to have people running around looking for their seats while he is attempting to establish a "closed circuit" between himself and his listeners.

Sometimes an audience gets the impression that the performer is overrating himself. To avoid this, clearly show your gratitude: "I am so glad you liked my efforts." I repeat, show your gratitude.

THE AUDIENCE

One of the first questions that comes to the mind of the performer is: "What kind of a group am I going to sing for?" You don't have to sing exclusively nonserious or light music to a nonmusical audience; on the other hand, a music club or the students of a college of music do not necessarily need an all-Purcell or all-Schubert program. To a certain extent, though, you should adjust your program to the audience. During the Occupation of Denmark by the Germans during World War II, ever-growing crowds of Danes gathered to hear their national folk songs. These were not typical concertgoers or music connoisseurs; they were simply Danes who wanted and needed to manifest their national feelings. It would have been wrong and slightly tactless to sing Wagner or Brahms to such an audience. Those in the audience at a political meeting want to hear the songs that agree with their political convictions. They would be slightly confused if they had to listen to *La Bonne Chanson* by Fauré, or Samuel Barber's *Hermit Songs*. A third kind of nonmusical audience is the social gathering. Traditionally, they want some kind of entertainment, and it does not matter too much whether this is supplied by a comedian, a violinist, or a beautifully dressed soprano. It can be terribly frustrating to perform for an audience that has gathered because it is "the thing to do," or because it gives everybody a feeling that "we belong." A well-known German Lieder singer presented the *Winterreise* cycle to such an audience once. He sang it without intermission, so the poor dressed-up crowd had no chance to show off their fancy clothes or indulge in social small talk, which was one of the principal reasons they had come.

The musical audience, the audience of true music lovers who cannot exist without good music, is not very large numerically, but it is one of the goals of the serious singer to urge more and more people into this camp and to educate people to appreciate listening to the live performance of great musical compositions.

THE CRITICS

The musical world is dependent on music criticism; this is, on the whole, a healthy situation. Reviews play a role in the artist's life, as well as in the public evaluation of his performance, that is almost frightening. The music critics possess an enormous power and a grave responsibility at the same time. Even in this time of radio and television there is an implicit belief in the printed word: "It says so in the newspapers, so there must be some truth in it." The music critic guides and even shapes the public opinion, and thus the artist is dependent on the views the critic expresses.

Artist and critic should fight for the same causes, and not be adversaries. On the other hand, camaraderie or too close a relationship between the artist and the critic should be avoided in order to prevent *any* suggestion of corruption.

In his review, the music critic should report the reaction of the audience. Too often the performer is disappointed when he finds no reference to this in the review. Too often the fifty thousand who read about the recital in the paper do not understand that the five hundred who were present in the hall enjoyed the concert more than the reviewer did. But remember, *no one asked us to take up a singing career*. We must humbly accept both positive and negative reactions from both the audience and the critics. All we can hope for is fair and constructive criticism that will help us in charting our path.

Do not let yourself be too closely influenced by what the newspapers say. There are some reviews that you cherish so much that you keep them in your billfold until they are worn and crumpled. There are others that make you furious and desperate. I am acquainted with both kinds from personal experience. If you concentrate on improving yourself constantly, the latter should not be decisive. It is my firm belief that your artistic career is neither ruined nor "made" by music critics.

RECORDED MUSIC

The progress that has been made in recent years in our ability to record music is truly impressive. To have marvelous artists who are not with us any more (Melba, Ferrier, Flagstad, Caruso, Melchior, Schipa, Chaliapin, Pinza, and many others) come right into our living rooms and sing for us is certainly something of a miracle. An enormous amount of music has been recorded, and this treasure has widened the musical audience to previously unheard-of numbers. Technical reproduction, however, is not the final goal of a singer. Though recordings have a great educational value, if they are not used in the proper way, the listener may become passive, letting the sound pour into his ears without reacting to it intellectually. He hears, but he does not listen!

The human rapport to which both singer and listener are exposed in a live performance is a necessity for most people. "Canned" music will never produce the magnetic tension that one can sometimes experience in the concert hall. Still, there are many people who prefer to sit in their rockers in front of the fireplace and listen to recordings of their own choice. However tempting it may be to choose the artist you prefer, the music you feel like listening to at the moment, and the length of time you wish to listen, there is something you will automatically miss: the close contact of the live performance.

There is always the danger that the music emitting from the phonograph, the radio, or the television set may become only background sounds to which you talk, eat, telephone, and even work. You no longer concentrate on it or analyze it. You merely hear it.

Both the student and the experienced singer should listen to recordings to become familiar with the musical literature, but it is a serious and much too common mistake to think that vocal technique or sound production can be learned from a recording. Your ideas about phrasing and interpretation cannot be learned from the artist on the record. Only after you work out your own interpretation of a composition are you prepared to listen to another's interpretation. By establishing an active and critical manner of listening, you will avoid being guilty of impersonal and cheap imitations.

Appendix I

International Phonetic Association Symbols

VOWELS

SYMBOL	ENGLISH	ITALIAN	GERMAN	FRENCH
[æ]	hat [hæt]	——	——	——
[a]	mine [main]	——	hatte ['hatə]	amour [amu:ʀ]
[ɑ]	father ['fɑ:ðə]	caro ['kɑ:ro]	Vater ['fɑ:təʀ]	âme [ɑ:m]
[ɑ̃]	——	——	——	lampe [lɑ̃:p]
[e]	date [deit]	strega ['stre:gɑ]	ewig ['e:vɪç]	été [ete]
[ɛ]	debt [dɛt]	bello ['bɛl:lo]	setzen ['sɛtsən]	aimer [ɛme]
[ə]	towel ['tɑʊəl]	——	haben ['hɑ:bən]	venir [vəni:ʀ]
[ɛ̃]	——	——	——	fin [fɛ̃]
[i]	heat [hi:t]	lira ['li:rɑ]	bieten ['bi:tən]	rire [ʀi:ʀ]
[ɪ]	hit [hɪt]	——	bitten ['bɪtən]	——
[o]	coal [koʊl]	amore [ɑ'mo:re]	Ofen ['o:fən]	rose [ʀo:z]

Symbol	English	Italian	German	French
[ɔ]	spot [spɔt]	forte ['fɔrte]	offen ['ɔfən]	homme [ɔm]
[õ]	——	——	——	onze [õz]
[ø]	——	——	König ['køniç]	peu [pø]
[œ]	fur [fœ:]	——	können ['kœnən]	peur [pœ:ʀ]
[œ̃]	——	——	——	parfum [paʀfœ̃]
[u]	pool [pu:l]	luna ['lu:nɑ]	Mut [mu:t]	jour [ʒu:ʀ]
[ʊ]	pull [pʊl]	——	Mutter ['mʊtəʀ]	——
[ʌ]	but [bʌt]	——	——	——
[ ]	——	——	fühlen ['fy:ən]	lune [lyn]
[ ]	——		füllen ['fʏlən]	——

DIPHTHONGS

Symbol	English	Italian	German	French
[ɑi]	find [faɪnd]	mai [mɑi]	Eis [ɑɪs]	——
[ɑʊ]	house [hɑʊs]	aura ['ɑʊrɑ]	Haus [hɑʊs]	——
[ɛə]	chair [tʃɛə]	——	——	——
[eɪ]	name [neɪm]	——	——	——
[ɛɪ]	——	miei [mjɛɪ]	——	——
[ɪə]	hear [hɪə]	——	——	——
[ɔɪ]	boy [bɔɪ]	suoi [swɔi]	heulen ['hɔɪlən]	——
[oʊ]	go [goʊ]	——	——	——

CONSONANTS

Symbol	English	Italian	German	French
[b]	bat [bæt]	bella ['bɛl:lɑ]	Baum [baʊm]	beau [bo]
[d]	do [du:]	dona ['do:nɑ]	du [du:]	doux [du]
[dʒ]	judge [dʒʌdʒ]	gentile [dʒɛn'ti:lə]	——	——
[tʃ]	chair [tʃɛə]	cento ['tʃɛnto]	——	——
[f]	full [fʊl]	flora ['flɔ:rɑ]	Fisch [fɪʃ]	phrase [fʀa:z]
[g]	goose [gu:s]	gloria ['glɔrjɑ]	gehen ['ge:ən]	gare [ga:ʀ]
[h]	ham [hæ:m]	——	Herz [hɛʀts]	haine [(h)ɛ:n] (weakly aspirated)
[j]	young [jʌŋ]	pianto ['pjɑnto]	ja [ja:]	bien [bjɛ̃]
[ç]	——	——	ich [ɪç]	——
[k]	cool [ku:l]	carta ['kɑrtɑ]	kühl [kʏ:l]	café [kafe]
[l]	live [lɪv]	larva ['lɑrvɑ]	leben ['le:bən]	lit [li]
[ʎ]	——	fogli ['foʎi]	——	——
[m]	mat [mæt]	mamma [mɑm:mɑ]	mehr [me:ʀ]	mère [mɛʀ]

Symbol	English	Italian	German	French
[n]	now [nɑ̃ʊ]	nome ['no:me]	nun [nu:n]	nature [naty:ʀ]
[ŋ]	singer ['sɪŋə]	angolo ['ɑŋgolo]	bange ['baŋə]	——
[ɲ]	——	ogni ['ɔɲ'i]	——	champagne [ʃɑ̃paɲ]
[p]	place [pleɪs]	padre ['pɑ:dre]	Perle ['pɛʀlə]	petit [pəti]
[r]	rose [roʊz]	rosa ['rɔ:zɑ]	——	——
[ʀ]	——	——	Rose ['ʀo:zə]	rose [ʀo:z]
[ɹ]	river ['ɹɪvəɹ] (American)	——	——	——
[x]	——	——	ach [ɑ:x]	——
[s]	sea [si:]	santa ['sɑntɑ]	essen ['ɛsən]	salle [sal]
[z]	zero ['ziəroʊ]	casa ['kɑ:zɑ]	singen ['zɪŋən]	maison [mɛzõ]
[ʃ]	show [ʃoʊ]	scena ['ʃe:nɑ]	stehen ['ʃte:ən]	chambre [ʃɑ̃:bʀ]
[ʒ]	azure ['æʒʊə]	——	——	joli [ʒoli]
[t]	top [tɔp]	terra ['tɛr:rɑ]	Tür [tʏ:ʀ]	table [tabl]
[θ]	thin [θɪn]	——	——	——
[ð]	this [ðɪs]	——	——	——
[v]	very ['verɪ]	vita ['vitɑ]	war [vɑ:ʀ]	avec [avɛk]
[w]	we [wi:]	Guido ['gwi:do]	——	moi [mwa]
[ʍ]	where [ʍɛə]	——	——	——

To indicate where the stress in a word falls, an apostrophe is placed before the accented syllable, e.g., *apostrophe* [ə'pɔstrəfɪ]. To indicate a long sound, a colon is placed after the vowel, e.g., *fool* [fu:l], or between double consonants, as in the Italian *tranquillo* [trɑŋkwil:lo]. To indicate a nasal vowel, a tilde [~] is placed over the vowel, as the French *enfin* [ɑ̃fɛ̃].

Appendix II
Recommended Listening

THE ART SONG

Beethoven, Ludwig van: *An die ferne Geliebte*
Fischer-Dieskau, Demus acc. DGG 139197 stereo

Berlioz, Hector: *Nuits d'Été*
Crespin, Ansermet, conductor London 25821 stereo

Brahms, Johannes: *Ein Johannes Brahms Liederabend*
Fischer-Dieskau, Demus acc. DGG 138011 stereo

Britten, Benjamin: *Canticles I, II, and III*
Pears, Hahessy, Tuckwell, Britten London OS 25332 stereo
Serenade for Tenor, Horns, and Strings
Pears, Tuckwell, Britten London CS 6398 stereo

Debussy, Claude: *Beau Soir* and *Romance*, etc.
Teyte, Moore acc. Angel COLH 134, mono only
or
Souzay, Baldwin acc. DGG 138758 stereo
Les Cloches (from *Deux Romances*)
Souzay, Baldwin acc. DGG 138758 stereo
Fantoches and *Ballade des Femmes de Paris*
Teyte, Cortot acc. Angel COLH 134, mono only

Dowland, John: *Lute Songs*
Pears, Bream acc. Victor LSC 2819 stereo

Duparc, Henri: *Chanson Triste, Invitation au Voyage*
Teyte, Moore acc. Angel COLH 138, mono only

Fauré, Gabriel: *La Bonne Chanson*
Souzay, Baldwin acc. Epic BC1122 stereo

Grieg, Edvard: *Songs*

Flagstad London 25103 stereo

or

Flagstad Seraphim 60046, mono only

Haydn, Franz Joseph: *Canzonettas*

Pears, Britten acc. London 5687; 25321

Mahler, Gustav: *Kindertotenlieder*

Fischer-Dieskau, Böhm, conductor DGG 138879 stereo

Lieder eines fahrenden Gesellen

Fischer-Dieskau, Furtwängler, conductor Angel 35522, mono only

Mozart, Wolfgang Amadeus: *Das Veilchen*

Schwarzkopf, Gieseking acc. Angel 35270, mono only

Poulenc, Francis: *Banalités*

Bernac, Poulenc acc. 2-Odyssey 32260009, mono only

or

Kruysen Westminster 17105 stereo

Le Bestiare

Kruysen Westminster 17105 stereo

Purcell, Henry: *Songs*

Deller, Leonhardt acc. Bach Guild 547, mono only

Ravel, Maurice: *Don Quichotte à Dulcinée*

Souzay, Vandernoot cond. Imported Pathé 30330, mono only

Shéhérazade

Crespin, Ansermet, conductor London 25821 stereo

or

Tourel, Bernstein, conductor Columbia CMS-6438

Schubert, Franz: *Die schöne Müllerin*

Wunderlich, Giesen acc. DGG 139219/20

or

Schiøtz, Moore acc. Imported Danish MOAK I, mono only

Winterreise
Fischer-Dieskau, Moore acc. Angel 3640/41
Der Doppelgänger
Fischer-Dieskau, Moore acc. Angel 36127 stereo
Frühlingsglaube
Wunderlich, Giesen acc. DGG 139219-20 stereo
Die Stadt
Fischer-Dieskau, Moore acc. Angel 36127 stereo
Wanderers Nachtlied
Fischer-Dieskau, Demus acc. DGG 138117 stereo

Schumann, Robert: *Der arme Peter*, I–III
Kruysen, Richard acc. Valois/MB942 stereo
Dichterliebe, opus 48
Wunderlich, Giesen acc. DGG 139125 stereo
Frauenliebe und -leben, opus 42
Baker, Isepp acc. Saga XID 5277 stereo
Liederkreis, opus 39
Fischer-Dieskau, Moore acc. Angel 36266 stereo
Die Lotosblume (from *Myrthen*)
Fischer-Dieskau, Demus acc. DGG 138655 stereo

Sibelius, Jean: *Songs*
Björling, var. acc. Victor LM 1771, mono only
or
Björling, var. acc. Victor LM 2784, mono only
or
Nilsson, Bokstedt acc. London 25942 stereo

Strauss, Richard: *Vier letzte Lieder* (and five other songs)
Schwarzkopf, Szell, conductor Angel 36347 stereo

Wolf, Hugo: *Italienisches Liederbuch*
Seefried, Fischer-Dieskau; Werba,
Demus acc. DGG 18568/69 mono only

Schwarzkopf, Moore acc. (excerpts) Angel 35883, mono only

Goethe Lieder

Fischer-Dieskau, Moore acc. Electrola 91072/73 stereo

Mörike Lieder

Prey, Moore acc. London 25946 stereo

Spanisches Liederbuch

Fischer-Dieskau, Schwarzkopf, Moore acc. Angel 35838 stereo

THE ORATORIO

Bach, Johann Sebastian: *Arias* (and Handel: Arias)

Ferrier, Boult, conductor London 5083 mono only

St. John Passion

Wunderlich, Fischer-Dieskau, Kohn, Forster, conductor HMV ASD526-28

or

Häfliger, Prey, Engen, Lear, Töpper, Richter, conductor 3-DGG ARC-198328/30 stereo

St. Matthew Passion

Stich-Randall, Rössl-Majdan, Ebrelius, Braun, Kmentt, Berry, Wöldike, conductor 4-Vanguard S-269/72

or

Laszlo, Rössl-Majdan, Cuénod, Munteanu, Scherchen, conductor 4-Westminster 4402

or

Schwarzkopf, Ludwig, Gedda, Pears, Fischer-Dieskau, Berry, Klemperer, conductor 5-Angel S-3599 stereo

Brahms, Johannes: *Ein deutsches Requiem*

Schwarzkopf, Fischer-Dieskau, Klemperer, conductor 2-Angel S-3624 stereo

Britten, Benjamin: *War Requiem*

Vishnevskaya, Fischer-Dieskau, Pears,
Britten, conductor 2-London 1255 stereo

Handel, George Frederick: *Messiah*
Addison, Oberlin, Lloyd, Warfield,
Bernstein, conductor 2-Columbia M2L-242/M2S-603 stereo

or

Harper, Watts, Wakefield, Shirley-Quirk,
Davis, conductor 3-Phillips PHS-3-992 stereo

Haydn, Franz Joseph: *Die Schöpfung*
Stich-Randall, Felbermayer, Dermota, Schöffler,
Guthrie, Wöldike, conductor Vanguard CK2 130/1

Mendelssohn, Felix: *Elijah*
Delman, Proctor, Maran, Boyce, Cunningham,
Krips, conductor 3-London 4315

Mozart, Wolfgang Amadeus: *Requiem*
Seefried, Tourel, Simoneau, Warfield,
Walter, conductor Columbia ML-5012

Penderecki, Krzysztof: *St. Luke Passion*
Woytowicz, Hiolski, Ladysz, Bartsch,
Czyz, conductor 2-Victor VIC(S)-6015 stereo

Verdi, Giuseppe: *Requiem*
Price, Elias, Bjoerling, Tozzi
Reiner, conductor 2-Victor LDS-6091 stereo

THE OPERA

Beethoven, Ludwig van: *Fidelio*
Ludwig, Vickers, Frick, Berry,
Klemperer, conductor 3-Angel 3625 stereo

Bellini, Vincenzo: *Norma*
Callas, Zaccaria, Corelli, Vincenzi,
Ludwig, Serafin, conductor 3-Angel 3615 stereo

Bizet, Georges: *Carmen*
Callas, Gedda, Massard, Guiot,
Prêtre, conductor 3-Angel 3650 stereo

or

Price, Corelli, Merrill, Freni,
Karajan, conductor 3-Victor LDS 6164 stereo

Cherubini, Luigi: *Medea*
Callas, Scotto, Picchi, Modesti, Pirazinni,
Serafin, conductor 3-Mercury SR 3-9000 stereo

Debussy, Claude: *Pelléas et Mélisande*
De los Angeles, Jansen, Souzay,
Cluytens, conductor 3-Angel 3561, mono only

Gounod, Charles: *Faust*
De los Angeles, Gedda, Christoff, Berton,
Cluytens, conductor 4-Angel 3622 stereo

From *Faust*: "Le Veau d'Or"
and
"Vous Qui Faites l'Endormie"

Chaliapin Angel COLH 141, mono only

Massenet, Jules: *Manon*
De los Angeles, Legay, Notti, Dens,
Monteux, conductor 4-Capitol GDR 7171, mono only

Monteverdi, Claudio: *L'incoronazione di Poppea*
Zareska, Bückel, Ulrich-Mielsch, Burgess,
Ewerhardt, conductor 3-Vox SOPBX 5113 stereo

Mozart, Wolfgang Amadeus: *Così fan tutte*
Seefried, Merriman, Prey, Fischer-Dieskau,
Jochum, conductor DGG 138861/3 stereo

or

Souez, Helletsgrüber, Eisinger, Nash, Domgraf-Fassbänder, Brownlee, Busch, conductor (Glyndebourne Fest.) Turnabout 4120/2 mono only

Don Giovanni

Nilsson, Price, Valletti, Siepi, Corena, Ratti, Leinsdorf, conductor 4-Victor LSC 6410 stereo

or

Souez, Helletsgrüber, Pataky, Brownlee, Baccaloni, Busch, conductor (Glyndebourne Fest.) 3-Turnabout 4117/9, mono only

Die Entführung aus dem Serail

Marshall, Hollweg, Simoneau, Beecham, conductor 2-Angel S3555 stereo

Le Nozze di Figaro

Mildmay, Helletsgrüber, Rautavaara, Domgraf-Fassbänder, Henderson, Tajo, Busch, conductor (Glyndebourne Fest.) 3-Turnabout 4114/6, mono only

or

Seefried, Stader, Töpper, Fischer-Dieskau, Capecchi, Fricsay, conductor DGG 138697/9 stereo

or

Moffo, Schwarzkopf, Wächter, Taddei, Giulini, conductor 4-Angel 3608 stereo

Die Zauberflöte

Stader, Streich, Häfliger, Fischer-Dieskau, Greindl, Fricsay, conductor Heliodor 250573-3, mono only

or

Lear, Peters, Otto, Wunderlich, Fischer-Dieskau, Böhm, conductor DGG 138981/3 stereo

or

Janowitz, Popp, Ludwig, Berry, Gedda, Frick,
Klemperer conductor — 3-Angel 3651 stereo

Puccini, Giacomo: *La Bohème*
Freni, Gedda, Sereni, Mazzoli, Basiola,
Adani, Schippers, conductor — 2-Angel 3643 stereo

Madama Butterfly
De los Angeles, Björling, Pirazzini, Sereni,
Santini, conductor — 3-Angel 3604 stereo

Rossini, Gioacchino: *Il Barbiere di Seviglia*
Peters, Merrill, Valletti, Tozzi,
Leinsdorf, conductor — 3-Victor LSC 6143 stereo

or

Callas, Gobbi, Alva, Zaccaria,
Galliera, conductor — 3-Angel 3559 stereo

Strauss, Richard: *Der Rosenkavalier*
Schwarzkopf, Ludwig, Stich-Randall, Edelmann,
Wächter, Karajan, conductor — 4-Angel 3563 stereo

Verdi, Giuseppe: *Aida*
Price, Gorr, Vickers, Tozzi,
Solti, conductor — 3-Victor LSC 6158 stereo

or

Nilsson, Bumbry, Corelli,
Mehta, conductor — 3-Angel 3716 stereo

Falstaff
Ligabue, Sciutti, Resnik, Oncina,
Fischer-Dieskau, Panerai,
Bernstein, conductor — Columbia M3S750 stereo

Otello
Rysanek, Vickers, Gobbi,
Serafin, conductor — 3-Victor LDS 6155 stereo

Wagner, Richard: *Lohengrin*

Grümmer, Ludwig, Thomas, Fischer-Dieskau,
Wiener, Frick, Kempe, conductor 5-Angel 3641 stereo

Die Meistersinger

Grümmer, Shock, Frantz,
Kempe, conductor 5-Angel 3572, mono only

Weber, Karl Maria von: *Der Freischütz*

Seefried, Streich, Holm, Wächter, Böhme,
Jochum, conductor DGG 13869/40 stereo

From *Der Freischütz,*
"Leise, leise, fromme Weise"

Lotte Lehmann Angel COLH 112, mono only

Appendix III

List of Aksel Schiøtz Recordings

Franz Schubert: *Die schöne Müllerin* ODEON MOAK 1
With Gerald Moore

Opera and Oratorio ODEON MOAK 2

Dietrich Buxtehude: "Aperite mihi" Terzet (A.T.B.)
Mogens Wöldike, harpsichord

George Frederick Handel: "Comfort ye" and "Every valley" from *Messiah*
Mogens Wöldike, conductor

Johann Sebastian Bach: "O, Schmerz" and "Ich will bei meinem Jesu wachen" from *Matthäuspassion*
Mogens Wöldike, conductor

Franz Joseph Haydn: "Mit Würd und Hoheit" from *Die Schöpfung*
Mogens Wöldike, conductor

Wolfgang Amadeus Mozart: "Dies Bildnis" from *Die Zauberflöte*
"Dalla sua pace" from *Don Giovanni*
"Il mio tesoro" from *Don Giovanni*
"Hier soll ich dich denn sehen" from *Die Entführung*
"Im Mohrenland" from *Die Entführung*

"Un' aura amorosa"
from *Così fan tutte*

Egisto Tango, conductor

The Romantic Era ODEON MOAK 3

Robert Schumann: "Dichterliebe" I–XVI
Johannes Brahms: "Die Mainacht"
"Sonntag"
"Der Mond steht über dem Berge"
With Gerald Moore
Edvard Grieg: "Jeg elsker dig"
"To brune øjne"
With Folmer Jensen
"Vær hilset, I damer"
"Forårsregn"
With Gerald Moore
Niels Wilhelm Gade: "Knud Lavard"
"Hvorfor svulmer Weichselfloden?"
With Herman D. Koppel
Olufs Ballade from "Elverskud"
Mogens Wöldike, conductor

C. E. F. Weyse and Carl Nielsen ODEON MOAK 4

C. E. F. Weyse: "Nu vågne alle Guds fugle små"
"Lysets engel går med glans"
"Gud ske tak og lov"
"I fjerne kirketårne hist"
"Bliv hos os, når dagen hælder"
"Der står et slot i Vesterled"
"Natten er så stille"
"Kommer hid, I piger små"

"Duftende enge og kornrige vange"
"Skøn jomfru"

With Folmer Jensen and Herman D. Koppel

Carl Nielsen: "Jens Vejmand"
"Grøn er vårens hæk"
"Sommersang"
"I aften"
"Irmelin Rose"
"Den milde dag"
"I solen går jeg bag min plov"
"Underlige aftenlufte"
"Jeg bærer med smil min byrde"
"Så bittert var mit hjerte"

With Chr. Christiansen and Herman D. Koppel, Orchestra conductors: Sv. Chr. Felumb and J. Hye-Knudsen

Popular Danish Songs and Bellman Songs ODEON MOAK 5

O. Ring: "Danmark, nu blunder den lyse nat"
Danish Folk Melody: "Det haver så nyligen regnet"
K. Riisager: "Mor Danmark"
O. Mortensen: "Du danske sommer"
P. E. Lange-Müller: "Midsommervise"
P. Heise: "Ørnen løfter ned stærke slag"
V. Bendix: "Hvor tindrer nu min stjerne"
J. P. E. Hartmann: "Du, som har sorg i sinde"
K. Vad Thomsen: "Til glæden"
J. P. E. Hartmann: "Lær mig, nattens stejrne"
C. M. Bellman: "Käraste bröder, systrar och vänner"
"Gubben är gammal"

"Ulla, min Ulla"
"Vila vid denna källa"
"Hör klockorna med ängsligt dån"
"Så lunka vi så småningom"
"Joachim uti Babylon"
"Fjäriln vingad syns på Haga"

The Art of Aksel Schiøtz ODEON MOAK 19

Dietrich Buxtehude: "Was mich auf dieser Welt betrübt"
Johann Sebastian Bach: "Frohe Hirten, eilt, ach eilet" from *Christmas Oratorio*
J. P. E. Hartmann: Sverkels Romance from *Liden Kirsten*
Tavlebordsduet from *Liden Kirsten*
Charles Gounod: "Vær hilset, plet" from *Faust*
P. Tchaikovsky: "Hvorfor er du forsvunden," and "Fremtid har liv og død i eje," from *Eugen Onegin*
J. P. E. Hartmann: "Den kedsom vinter gik sin gang"
P. Heise: "Skovensomhed"
"Til en veninde"
"Aften på loggiaen"
P. E. Lange-Müller: "Serenade" from "Der var engang"
Carl Nielsen: "Genrebillede"
"Jægersang"
"Vi, sletternes sønner"
With various accompanists

The Art of Aksel Schiøtz ODEON MOAK 20

Danish Medieval Songs: "Dronning Dagmars død"
"Lave og Jon"
"Ebbe Skammelsøn"
"Ulver og Vænelil"
John Dowland: "Flow, My Tears"

"Shall I sue"
"Now Cease, My Wand'ring Eyes"
Edvard Grieg: "Ved Ronderne"
"En digters sidste sang"
B. Sjöberg: "Den förste gång, jag såg dig"
Maurice Ravel: "Don Quichotte à Dulcinée" I–III
Swedish Folk melody: "Jeg gik mig ud en sommerdag"
C. E. F. Weyse: "En skål for den mø"
H. Rung: "Modersmålet"
T. Lamb: "Aftensuk"
T. Aagaard: "Jeg ser de bøgelyse øer"
O. Ring: "Sig, nærmer tiden"
A. Agerby: "Havren"
S. E. Tarp: "Her har hjertet hjemme"
P. Hamburger: "Sne"
O. Mortensen: "Min skat"
With various accompanists

The above records are available from Peter's International, 600 Eighth Avenue, New York, N.Y.

Franz Schubert: "Liebesbotschaft" Dyer-Bennet Records
"Ganymed" DYBXS 2
"Der Wanderer an den Mond"
"An die Laute"
C. M. Bellman: "Blåsen nu alla"
"Opp, Amaryllis"
"Drick ur ditt glas"
Hugo Wolf: "Heb auf dein blondes Haupt"
"Der Tambour"
"Verschwiegene Liebe"
"Auf dem grünen Balkon"
"Anakreons Grab"

Johannes Brahms: "An die Nachtigall"
"Im Waldeseinsamkeit"
"Mein Mädel hat einen Rosenmund"
With Paul Ulanowsky and Richard Dyer-Bennet

The above is available from Dyer-Bennet Records, Box 235, Woodside, N.Y.

The Art of Aksel Schiøtz

Album 1: Fourteen Songs of Carl Nielsen Seraphim 60112

"Den milde Dag" from *Fynsk Foraar*
"Saa bittert var mit Hjerte"
"Jens Vejmand"
"Grøn er Vaarens Hæk"
"Sommersang"
"I aften"
"Irmelin Rose"
"I Solen gaar jeg bag min Plov"
"Min Pige er saa lys som Rav"
"Jeg bærer med Smil min Byrde"
"Underlige Aftenlufte"
"Pagen højt paa taarnet sad"
"Vi sletternes sønner"
"Glenten styrter fra fjeldets kam"
With Chr. Christiansen and Herman D. Koppel,
Orchestra conductors: Sv. Chr. Felumb and J. Hye-Knudsen

A complete discography of Aksel Schiøtz recordings has been published by "Nationaldiskoteket," Copenhagen, Denmark, 1966, and will be mailed upon request (use international postage coupons of 50 cents).

Bibliography

Adler, Kurt. *The Art of Accompanying and Coaching.* Minneapolis: University of Minnesota Press, 1965.

Arnholtz, Arthur. *Om Sangforedrag* (On Song Interpretation). Copenhagen: Engstrøm & Sødring, 1946.

Britten, Benjamin. "On Winning the First Aspen Award," *Saturday Review* (August 22, 1964).

Capell, Richard. *Schubert's Songs.* New York: Basic Books, Inc., 1957.

Coffin, Burton. *Phonetic Readings.* Boulder, Colorado: Pruett Press, 1964.

Croiza, Claire. *Un Art de l'Interpretation.* Edited by Hélène Abraham. Paris: Office de Centralisation d'Ouvrages, 1954.

Dorian, Frederick. *History of Music in Performance.* New York: W. W. Norton & Company, Inc., 1942.

Errolle, Ralph. *Italian Diction for Singers.* Boulder, Colorado: Pruett Press, 1963.

Goldman, A., and Sprinchorn, E. *Wagner on Music and Drama,* A Compendium of Richard Wagner's Prose Works. New York: E. P. Dutton & Co., Inc., 1964.

Grout, Donald J. *A Short History of the Opera.* New York: Columbia University Press, 1965.

Greene, Harry Plunket. *Interpretation in Song.* Lonon: Macmillan & Co., Ltd., 1956.

Hall, David. *The Record Book.* New York: Oliver Durrell, Inc., 1948.

———. *Records.* New York: Alfred A. Knopf, Inc., 1950.

Hall, David, and Levin, Abner. *The Disc Book.* New York: Long Playing Publications, 1955.

Hanslick, Eduard. *Music Criticisms 1846–1899,* ed. Henry Pleasants. Baltimore, Maryland: Peregrine, 1963.

Jeppesen, Knud. *La Flora.* Copenhagen: Wilhelm Hansen, 1949, Vols. I–III.

Kagen, Sergius. *Music for the Voice.* New York: Holt, Rinehart and Winston, Inc., 1949.

Kerman, Joseph. *Opera as Drama.* New York: Alfred A. Knopf, Inc., 1956.

Kolodin, Irving. *Guide to Recorded Music.* New York: Doubleday & Company, Inc., 1950.

———. *The Composer as Listener.* New York: Horizon, 1958.

Lang, Paul Henry. *Music in Western Civilization.* New York: W. W. Norton & Company, Inc., 1941.

———. *George Frederic Handel.* New York: W. W. Norton & Company, Inc., 1966.

Lehmann, Lotte. *More than Singing, The Interpretation of Song.* New York: Boosey & Hawkes, Inc., 1945.

McClusky, David Blair. *Your Voice at Its Best.* Plymouth, Mass.: Memorial Press, 1967.

Miller, Philip L. *The Ring of Words.* New York: Doubleday & Company, Inc., 1963.

———. *Guide to Long-Play Records—Vocal Music.* New York: Alfred A. Knopf, Inc., 1955.

Moore, Gerald. *The Unashamed Accompanist.* London: Ascherberg, 1964.

———. *Am I too Loud?* New York: Macmillan Company, 1963.

Northcote, Sydney. *Byrd to Britten; A Survey of English Song.* New York: Roz, 1966.

Newman, Ernest. *Stories of the Great Operas.* New York: Alfred A. Knopf, Inc., 1930.

———. *More Stories of Famous Operas.* New York: Alfred A. Knopf, Inc., 1943.

Panzéra, Charles. *L'Art de Chanter.* Paris: Edition Littéraires, 1945.

Prawer, Siegbert. *The Penguin Book of Lieder.* Baltimore, Maryland: Penguin Books, Inc., 1964.

Sachs, Curt. "The Road to Major." *The Musical Quarterly,* XXIX (1943), 403.

Sams, Eric. *The Songs of Hugo Wolf.* London: Dent, 1951.

Schering, Arnold. *Geschichte des Oratoriums.* Leipzig, Germany: Breitkopf & Härtel, 1911.

Shaw, Bernard. *Shaw on Music,* ed. Eric Bentley. New York: Doubleday & Company, Inc., 1955.

Siebs, Theodore. *Deutsche Hochsprache.* Berlin: Gruyter & Co., 1961.

Vennard, William. *Singing: The Mechanism and the Technic.* 3d ed. Los Angeles: University of California, 1964.

Walker, Frank. *Hugo Wolf.* New York: Alfred A. Knopf, Inc., 1952.

INDEX

D

E

F

G

H

I

R

S

T

U

V

W

Z

ABOUT THE AUTHOR

Aksel Schiøtz, the beloved Danish singer, was decorated by the late King Christian X for his services as "The Resistance Singer" during the Nazi occupation of Denmark. He has an international reputation in opera and concert. His Lieder recordings are a model for all singers. His *Die schöne Müllerin* is considered by many to be the finest record yet issued of this Schubert song cycle. He has performed Beethoven, Schubert, Schumann, Brahms, and Hugo Wolf Lieder and Scandinavian songs at the Edinburgh Festival, the Casals Festival at Perpignan, the Vancouver International Festival, and the Stratford Ontario Shakespeare Festival, and on numerous tours in Europe, the United States, and Canada. From 1955 to 1958, he was professor at the University of Minnesota. In 1958, he was appointed professor of voice at the Royal Conservatory of Music, University of Toronto. He left there to join the faculty of the University of Colorado, where he taught until 1968. In 1968 the Danish government offered him a professorship in Copenhagen.

70 71 72 73 10 9 8 7 6 5 4 3 2 1